30-Day Self-Esteem Reset for Men

A Daily Action Plan, Build Real Confidence, Set Strong Boundaries, Develop Healthier Relationships & Create Lasting Self-Trust

George Munson

GL DIGITAL PUBLISHING LLC

First Edition 2026

Contents

Introduction

You Do Not Need More Hype, You Need Evidence

If you're like many men looking to build real self-esteem, you've probably seen motivational videos, attended energetic seminars, or tried daily affirmations. Maybe you've stood in front of the mirror saying, "I *am a powerful, unstoppable force*" or "*I deserve success and happiness.*" Still, you might hear a quiet voice inside asking, Who are you trying to fool?

The truth is, your brain quickly notices when your words don't match your reality. It won't accept empty claims. Real self-esteem and confidence come from actions, not just talk. When you keep promises to yourself, finish tough tasks, or handle setbacks, you give your brain real proof that you can rely on yourself. That's the difference between hype and self-trust. Self-trust is built from your own track record.

This book gives you a clear, 30-day action plan to help you build real proof of self-trust. The goal is simple: show you that self-trust comes from repeated actions, not hype. You won't find big, unrealistic changes or pressure to act loud and dominant. Instead, the plan is about steady self-trust, small steps, and clear boundaries. When you prioritize your actions over fleeting feelings, you'll start to see real evidence that you can count on yourself.

The Stories of Ethan and Marcus

To see how self-esteem is built or lost, let's look at two men: Ethan Brooks and Marcus Reed. Both face everyday challenges, and both get stuck in habits that weaken their self-trust.

Ethan Brooks's Beat

Ethan Brooks is twenty-eight years old and works from home as a software support specialist. For the past three days, Ethan has spent his evenings swiping through a popular dating app. He put care into his profile, choosing clear photos and writing an honest bio. Despite this, his screen remains silent. After seventy-two hours, he has received zero matches.

Ethan sits on his couch, staring at the empty screen, feeling a familiar heaviness in his chest. He doesn't just see no matches; he takes it as a final judgment on his worth. His mind races with thoughts like: I'm unattractive. I'm socially awkward. I'll always be alone. This kind of thinking, called personalization and overgeneralization, turns a simple lack of matches into a painful belief about his whole life.

To deal with the pain, Ethan orders a big meal he hadn't planned on and spends hours scrolling through social media. He skips his plan to study for a new certification. By seeing an outside result as a judgment on who he is, Ethan gives up on his own goals and makes his self-doubt stronger.

Marcus Reed's Beat

Marcus Reed is forty-five years old, recently divorced, and works as a senior project analyst. For months, Marcus has worked late, covered extra shifts, and quietly assumed he was next in line for a promotion to director of operations. On a Friday afternoon, his department head calls a meeting and announces that a younger, newer colleague has been selected for the role.

On the outside, Marcus smiles, nods, and shakes his colleague's hand. He says what's expected so no one sees his disappointment. Inside, though, he feels a deep sense of shame. He doesn't see the decision as just business or a skills mismatch. Instead, he takes it as proof that he's no longer needed and that his best years are over.

When Marcus gets home, he sees a text from his ex-wife asking him to cancel his weekend plans and help her clean out her garage. He had planned to visit his brother, a trip he's already put off twice, but he quickly replies, "*Sure, I can help.*" Marcus thinks that by pleasing others and showing he's useful, he'll feel better about himself. Instead, he spends the weekend feeling quietly resentful, putting his own needs aside for short-term approval.

The Shared Pattern of Self-Abandonment

Even though Ethan and Marcus are at different points in life, they both fall into the same trap: turning one outside event into a sweeping judgment about themselves. This pattern is important because the 30-day plan is made to break it.

If you let outside results, ratings, or other people's choices decide your self-worth, you end up trying to manage your image or avoid risks to protect your ego. To break this cycle, start separating facts from feelings, and focus on actions that support your life, no matter how others react.

The Identity Verdict

To build self-trust, you need to know how your mind turns daily events into beliefs about yourself. This chapter explains the steps in that process, because that's where self-esteem is built or broken. Every day brings situations that test your expectations. How you move from an event to a belief about yourself shapes your self-esteem. This process has four parts: the Event, the Interpretation, the Emotional Response, and the Identity Verdict.

1. **What Happened (The Fact)**: The objective, observable reality that could be recorded on a camera. (e.g., "The client sent an email stating they chose a different vendor.")

2. **What I Felt (The Emotion)**: The immediate physical and emotional sensation. (e.g., A tightening in the stomach, disappointment, or anxiety.)

3. **What I Assumed (The Interpretation)**: The quick, automatic explanation your brain creates to make sense of the feeling. (e.g., "They chose someone else because my work is subpar.")

4. **The Global Identity Verdict (The Conclusion)**: The sweeping generalization you make about your character, intelligence, or future value. (e.g., "I am a bad businessman and will never succeed.")

The identity verdict is where the real harm happens. It's the habit of turning one event into a lasting label, and this book is here to help you stop that. Here are some common ways men turn simple events into harsh judgments:

- **The Event**: A woman declines an invitation to go out.
  The Verdict: *"Nobody wants me. I am fundamentally undesirable."*

- **The Event**: You make a formatting mistake on a presentation at work.
  The Verdict: *"I am incompetent. It is only a matter of time before I am fired."*

- **The Event**: A long-term marriage or relationship ends.
  The Verdict: *"I am a failure. I am incapable of being loved."*

- **The Event**: You step on the scale and realize you have gained ten pounds.
  The Verdict: *"I have completely let myself go. I have no discipline."*

- **The Event**: You feel a wave of physical anxiety before speaking in a meeting.
  The Verdict: "*I am weak. A capable man would not feel this way.*"

When you judge yourself by these identity verdicts, it feels like you're always on trial. Every conversation, email, or missed workout becomes proof you're not good enough. The 30-day plan will help you stop this pattern early so that you can see facts as helpful feedback instead of harsh judgments.

Worth Is Not the Same as Ranking

From early on, men are put into all kinds of ranking systems. Your sports skills, grades, college reputation, job title, income, and dating life measure you. Tracking these things can help you grow, but it's a big mistake to think your place in these rankings equals your worth as a person.

Consider the primary ranking systems that modern men use to measure their worth: career success, financial wealth, physical fitness, and social status.

- **Financial and Material Assets**: Comparing your salary, vehicle, home, or investment portfolio to those of your peers.

- **Physical Attributes**: Evaluating your height, hairline, muscularity, or body fat percentage against curated fitness media.

- **Dating and Social Validation**: Measuring your desirability by the number of matches on dating apps, the responsiveness of romantic interests, or active social invitations.

- **Professional Hierarchy**: Linking your entire identity to your job title, organizational level, or the size of the team you manage.

- **Performance Metrics**: Assessing your capability solely by your gym lift numbers, the pace of your run, or your productivity output.

If you base your self-esteem on these rankings, your sense of worth is never secure. If you get injured and can't lift weights, your confidence drops. If your business slows down, you feel lost. If your dating profile gets less attention, you start to feel invisible.

To build real confidence, you need to separate your progress in a skill from your value as a person. This is a key idea in this book. You can notice your sales are down this quarter (that's just a fact that needs a plan) without deciding you're worthless. Making this distinction helps you face challenges with a clear mind instead of feeling ashamed.

Core Rules of the 30-Day Plan

This plan isn't a bootcamp meant to wear you out, and it's not about hyping yourself up. It's a step-by-step way to gather real proof and build self-trust. To get the most from the next thirty days, follow these five main rules:

Rule 1: Keep It Small

Don't try to change your whole life at once. If your plan needs a lot of willpower, you'll probably give up on tough days. Make your promises so small they're almost impossible to miss. A ten-minute walk you finish is much better than a five-mile run you never start.

Rule 2: Focus on What You Control

Don't base your daily success on how others react to you. If your goal is to get a positive response from a cashier, you're letting a stranger decide your self-esteem, and they might just be having a bad day. But if your goal is to make eye contact and ask how their day is, you control the outcome.

Rule 3: No Empty Affirmations

You won't be told to say things you don't believe. If you feel anxious, you won't say, "I am filled with absolute confidence." Instead, you'll say, "I feel anxious, and I can still take my next step." We respect you too much to ask you to lie to yourself.

Rule 4: Run a Clean Restart

At some point in the next thirty days, you'll miss a target. When that happens, don't try to make up for it by working twice as hard the next day, and don't quit the plan. Missing once is just information. Notice what happened, adjust for any problems, and do the next small action right away.

Rule 5: Keep a Written Record

Your brain naturally focuses on mistakes and forgets small wins. To fight this, write down what you do each day. This written record is clear, solid proof of your progress.

Baseline Self-Esteem Assessments

Before you start the plan, take an honest look at where you are now. Answer the next questions as truthfully as you can. There are no right or wrong answers—just honest ones.

The Trust Inventory Assessment

On a scale of 1 (Never) to 5 (Always), rate how closely your daily behavior matches these statements:

1. When I set a personal goal (e.g., wake up early, exercise, work on a project), I follow through even if my motivation fades.
   Rating: _____

2. I can state my honest opinion or preference in a group setting without changing my mind to please others.
   Rating: _____

3. When someone pays me a sincere compliment, I can accept it with a simple "thank you" without deflecting or making a self-deprecating joke.
   Rating: _____

4. I can make an important decision without needing to poll my friends, family, or coworkers first.
   Rating: _____

5. When a plan fails, or I receive critical feedback, I can analyze the mistake without calling myself stupid or incompetent.
   Rating: _____

Total Score: _____ (Out of 25)

- **Score 5–12**: Your self-trust has been heavily eroded by consistent self-abandonment and external outsourcing. This 30-day plan will focus heavily on building small, unbreakable promises.

- **Score 13–19**: You have some areas of strength, but your confidence is likely highly dependent on external validation and performance metrics.

- **Score 20–25**: You possess a solid foundation of self-trust, and this plan will help you refine your boundaries and expand your actions into more challenging areas.

Identifying Your Primary Outsourcing Channel Assessment

Check the list below and pick the one area where you're most likely to let your self-worth depend on something outside yourself. Which one, if it went badly, would hurt your self-esteem the most?

- **Area A: Professional Status & Achievement** (Job titles, income, praise from superiors, productivity metrics)
- **Area B: Social & Romantic Approval** (Dating app success, partner's mood, size of friend group, text message response times)
- **Area C: Physical Presentation** (Hair loss, body composition, height, clothing style, signs of aging)
- **Area D: Performance & Capability** (Gym performance, skills, hobbies, intellect, needing to be the smartest person in the room)

Write down your primary outsourcing channel: ____________ (e.g., Area A, B, C, or D, and the specific trigger that most affects your self-worth).

As you go through this plan, pay extra attention to this area. Practice separating your sense of self from these outside factors.

The Commitment Contract

To start this program, read and sign the contract below. You're not promising to be perfect or never to feel afraid. You're promising to show up, take small steps, and support yourself even when things don't go as planned.

***

THE EVIDENCE-BASED SELF-ESTEEM CONTRACT

I, ____________________________, commit to engaging in this 30-day action plan starting on ________________.

By signing this document, I agree to the following terms with myself:

1. **I will prioritize action over feelings.** I accept that I do not need to feel confident, motivated, or fearless before I take a step. I will let my actions lead my emotions.

2. **I will keep my promises small.** I will not set unrealistic, massive goals that lead to burnout. I understand that building self-trust requires completing small, manageable tasks consistently.

3. **I will not lie to myself.** I will retire empty affirmations and toxic positivity. I will speak to myself with clear, objective, and realistic language.

4. **I will practice the clean restart.** If I miss a day or fail a specific challenge, I will not engage in self-punishment or abandon the program. I will take the next available micro-action.

5. **I will document my proof.** I will keep a written record of my daily practices, recognizing that my brain needs visible evidence to build lasting confidence.

Signed: ____________________

Date: _______________

***

You're now ready to begin. Turn the page to Chapter 1 and start Day 1 of your journey to real, evidence-based self-trust.

Chapter One

Stop Outsourcing Your Worth

Narrative Opening

Three days ago, Ethan Brooks downloaded a dating app, picked out his best photos, and wrote what he thought was a friendly, honest profile. Since then, he has checked the app many times, but the screen stays quiet. No notifications, no matches, no messages. Sitting on his bed in his quiet apartment, Ethan stares at his phone. He doesn't see this as just a slow start or a random result from the app. Instead, he takes it as proof that he is unattractive, awkward, and will always be alone. This outside result slips past his usual thinking and sticks to how he sees himself.

Across town, Marcus Reed stands in a bright office hallway. He just found out that a younger coworker got the promotion he thought would be his. On the outside, Marcus smiles, shakes hands, and gives polite congratulations. Inside, though, he feels a deep sense of shame. As he walks back to his desk, he doesn't think about company changes or how to improve for next time. Instead, he sees this missed promotion as proof that he is no longer needed, that he is a failure, and that his best years are behind him.

Both Ethan and Marcus are stuck in the same mental pattern: they turn something that happened on the outside into a sweeping judgment about who they are.

For Ethan, the cognitive chain is instantaneous:
External Event: No digital matches on a dating app.
Identity Verdict: "*I am undesirable and unlovable.*"

For Marcus, the sequence is identical:
External Event: A colleague receives a promotion.
Identity Verdict: "*I am valueless and obsolete.*"

In both stories, these men let outside systems decide their value: a dating app's algorithm and a company's management team. When they don't get the response they want, they feel powerless. Recognizing this can help you feel more in control and resilient, preventing your self-trust from falling apart.

The Identity Verdict

To break this harmful pattern, you first need to see how your mind creates an identity verdict. This happens when you take one outside event and let it define your whole character or worth. This shift happens quickly, often without you noticing:

[1. Observable Fact] -> [2. Emotional Sensation] -> [3. Subconscious Assumption] -> [4. Global Identity Verdict]

Let us dissect this chain step-by-step:

1. **The Observable Fact**: This is the raw, objective reality of what occurred, stripped of all adjectives, interpretations, and emotional weight. It is the data point that could be captured by a video camera or verified by an impartial third party. For example: The email contains a rejection letter.

2. **The Emotional Sensation**: Upon registering the fact, your nervous system reacts. You might feel a tightening in your chest,

a drop in your stomach, or a sudden flush of heat. This is a normal, biological response to disappointment or perceived social exclusion. For example: You feel a heavy sensation of sadness and anxiety.

3. **The Subconscious Assumption**: Because the human brain dislikes unresolved tension and seeks to explain physical discomfort, it quickly manufactures an explanation for the feeling. It links the external fact to a personal vulnerability. For example: The employer rejected my application because my skills are not good enough.

4. **The Global Identity Verdict**: This is the final, catastrophic leap. Instead of leaving the event as a specific failure or a localized setback, your mind uses it to issue a permanent ruling on your entire identity. For example: I am incompetent, and I will never have a successful career.

If you let this chain run its course, you develop what I call the Verdict Habit. Many men with low self-esteem fall into this by default. It shows up in everyday situations, where small events quickly turn into harsh judgments about yourself. Ask yourself: Have I ever automatically labeled myself based on a single event? Recognizing these patterns is the first step toward changing them.

- **The Social Scenario**:
  – **What happened**: You speak up at a gathering, and the group does not hear you or briefly talks over you.
  – **The Verdict**: "*I am invisible, socially awkward, and nobody cares what I have to say.*"

- **The Professional Scenario**:
  – **What happened**: You make a formatting error on a spreadsheet or miss a minor deadline.
  – **The Verdict**: "*I am a fraud, I am incompetent, and I am going to get fired.*"

- **The Relational Scenario**:
  – **What happened**: Your partner is quiet, distant, or tired after a long workday.
  – **The Verdict**: *"I am failing as a partner, and they are planning to leave me."*

- **The Physical Scenario**:
  – **What happened**: You look in the mirror and notice you have gained three pounds or your hair is thinning.
  – **The Verdict**: *"I have completely let myself go, and I am physically repulsive."*

- **The Internal Scenario**:
  – **What happened**: You feel a sudden wave of anxiety, self-doubt, or fear before a difficult presentation.
  – **The Verdict**: *"I am weak, cowardice runs in my veins, and a real man wouldn't feel this way."*

The problem with the Verdict Habit is that it makes it almost impossible to learn from feedback. If every mistake means you're not good enough, it's too painful to look at what went wrong. You might avoid hard tasks or get defensive instead. But if you can pause at the feeling stage and let the emotion pass without letting it define you, you keep the clear mind you need actually to improve.

Worth Is Not the Same as Ranking

From early on, men are taught to see life as a competition. You're shown different ways to measure how you stack up against others, and these rankings can be hard to resist because they give you a clear score or status of your investment and the zip code of your residence.

- **Financial & Career Rankings**: Annual income, job title, the prestige of your employer, the size of your investment portfolio, and the zip code of your residence.

- **Physical & Athletic Rankings**: Your bench press max, your body fat percentage, your height, your hair density, and how your physique compares to highly curated images on digital screens.
- **Social & Relational Rankings**: Dating app match rates, the physical attractiveness of your romantic partners, your total number of active friendships, and the volume of engagement on your social media posts.
- **Material Rankings**: The brand of car you drive, the watch on your wrist, and the sophistication of your hobbies or possessions.

When you accept these ranking systems, you make a big mistake: you mix up your **skills or status in one area** with **your basic worth as a person**.

Let us look at this distinction clearly. If you are a software engineer, you can have a skill ranking. You might be objectively better at writing clean code than a junior developer, and objectively less skilled than a principal engineer with twenty years of experience. This is a skill ranking. It is useful, measurable, and can be improved through deliberate practice.

However, your skill ranking as a software engineer has absolutely zero bearing on your intrinsic worth. A principal engineer does not possess more right to self-respect, dignity, and basic consideration than a junior engineer, a construction worker, or an unemployed person.

If you treat these rankings as a measure of your value, you end up chasing a finish line that keeps moving. For example, if you think, "*I'll respect myself when I make eighty thousand dollars a year*," as soon as you reach that, you notice others making even more. Your self-respect disappears again. The finish line always moves because there will always be someone with more money, strength, or status.

To build real self-trust, you need to look at your skills and situation honestly, but not let them define your whole self. You can notice that your fitness or savings aren't where you want them, without deciding you're a failure. When you stop tying your identity to these rankings, you free up energy to actually get better, instead of always worrying about where you stand.

Day 1: Find the Conditions You Have Placed on Respect

Today, your job is to uncover the hidden rules you've set for your own self-respect. Many men think they're working on self-improvement, but really, they're only accepting themselves if they hit certain outside goals. They set tough milestones and won't let themselves feel peace or dignity until they reach them.

Five-Minute Practice

Set a timer for five minutes. On paper or in your journal, finish the sentence below ten times. Don't overthink it, don't try to sound good, and don't write what you think you should say. Just write the honest expectations that come up for you each day:

***

I will finally respect myself when...

1. *I will finally respect myself when...* _______________
2. *I will finally respect myself when...* _______________
3. *I will finally respect myself when...* _______________
4. *I will finally respect myself when...* _______________
5. *I will finally respect myself when...* _______________

6. *I will finally respect myself when...* ______________
7. *I will finally respect myself when...* ______________
8. *I will finally respect myself when...* ______________
9. *I will finally respect myself when...* ______________
10. *I will finally respect myself when...* ______________

***

Action Step

Look over your list of ten. Read each one slowly. Then, **pick and circle the three that have the biggest effect on your daily life**, the ones that cause you the most stress, shame, or push you to overwork.

Workbook Prompt

After you've circled your top three, take some time to answer these questions:

1. How do these rules affect your relationships and your health?
2. What might your life look like if you let go of these demands and accepted yourself as you are?
3. What's one small thing you can do today to start separating your self-worth from these expectations?

Consider...

- **Origin**: Who taught you these three conditions? Was it a parent, a peer group, a former partner, or the societal messaging you consumed growing up?

- **The Moving Finish Line**: Have you achieved milestones in the past that you thought would grant you lasting self-respect, only to find that the feeling vanished within days or weeks? What did that experience teach you about the nature of external achievements?

- **The Cost**: What has this moving finish line cost you in terms of your peace of mind, your physical health, your relationships, and your willingness to try new things without the fear of being imperfect?

Day 2: Separate Facts From Verdicts

Your goal for Day 2 is to practice breaking down your emotions. Pick a tough or stressful situation in your life right now, and see how fast you turn simple facts into big judgments about yourself.

The Fact-Feeling-Verdict Worksheet

Copy this template into your journal and fill it out for one area where you feel stuck, rejected, or not good enough. This could be your job, dating life, a conflict with a friend, or your fitness:

1. **Observable Facts**: (Describe the situation using only raw, objective facts that could be verified by a third-party observer. No emotional language, no speculation, no adjectives like "terrible," "lazy," or "useless.")
   – *My input*: ________________

2. **Emotional Reaction**: (Identify the physical sensations and emotions you felt when this situation occurred. Use simple terms like fear, anger, sadness, shame, tight chest, or rapid heart rate.)
   – *My input*: ________________

3. **Identity Verdict**: (What is the dramatic, global story your mind

constructed about your character or future based on this event? What is the "I am..." statement?)
– *My input*: ________________

4. **Accurate Interpretation**: (What is a realistic, balanced view of the situation that acknowledges the difficulty but rejects the identity verdict? What are the alternative explanations?)
   – *My input*: ________________

5. **One Useful Next Action**: (What is one tiny, physical step you can take within your control to address the situation, regardless of how you feel?)
   – *My input*: ________________

Example Walkthrough

Here's an example of how to use this worksheet, based on a common work situation:

The Situation: My manager hasn't replied to my project proposal, and now I feel like I don't belong in this job.

1. **Observable Facts**: I sent a project proposal to my manager on Tuesday afternoon. It is now Friday morning, and I have received no response or acknowledgment of receipt.

2. **Emotional Reaction**: I feel a tight sensation in my chest, a sinking feeling in my stomach, and a general sense of anxiety and dread.

3. **Identity Verdict**: My manager thinks my proposal is incompetent, they regret hiring me, and I am a mediocre professional who is going to be passed over for any future opportunities.

4. **Accurate Interpretation**: I do not know why my manager has

not replied. They may be traveling, dealing with a high-priority crisis, or simply behind on email. My work history has been generally positive, and one unreturned email does not define my standing in this company.

5. **One Useful Next Action**: I will send a polite, one-sentence follow-up message asking if they need any adjustments to the proposal, and then I will focus on my next scheduled task.

Day 3: Make One Self-Directed Choice

When you let others decide your worth, you stop making choices based on what matters to you. Instead, you start hesitating all the time. You ask others for advice, check online, or wait for someone to tell you what to do, even for small things. This constant checking tells your mind that you don't trust yourself to make decisions.

Today, you'll build confidence by making one small decision on your own. Don't ask for permission, check with others, or look for outside approval.

Options for Your Self-Directed Choice

Choose one of the following micro-actions to execute today:

- **The Solo Menu Choice**: Order a meal or drink without asking anyone else what they are getting or what they recommend. Trust your first instinct.

- **The Style Statement**: Pick out an outfit, hairstyle, or accessory based entirely on how it makes you feel, without sending a photo to a friend for approval.

- **The Schedule Shift**: Rearrange one hour of your personal calendar today to do exactly what you want, without explaining or justifying the change to anyone else.

- **The Media Selection**: Choose a movie, book, or playlist to engage with tonight solely because it interests you, ignoring current trends or reviews.

- **Order Food Directly**: Go to a restaurant or cafe, look at the menu, and order what you genuinely want to eat within thirty seconds, without asking the server what they recommend, without checking online reviews of the dish, and without apologizing for your choice.

- **Decide Your Time**: Block out exactly one hour of your evening. Decide precisely how you will spend that hour (e.g., reading a book, organizing a drawer, walking in silence) and do it without asking anyone else if they mind, and without checking your phone for social cues.

- **Select Your Workout**: Choose a physical routine or walk route based solely on what your body needs today, rather than trying to find the "perfect, optimized, influencer-approved" training program online.

- **Wear What You Choose**: Select an item of clothing from your wardrobe that you enjoy wearing, but normally hesitate to put on because you worry what others might think of it. Wear it out into the world today without commenting on it or asking anyone's opinion.

- **Decline an Optional Invite**: If you have received an invite to a social gathering, digital call, or project meeting that is entirely optional and does not align with your energy or values today, decline it politely and immediately without manufacturing an elaborate excuse.

- **Choose a Project Direction**: Take one small task on your professional or personal to-do list, decide on the next step, and execute it using your best judgment, rather than waiting to ask a colleague or partner if they think it is the "right" way to do it.

After you've done your chosen action, write this Proof Statement in your journal:

> *"Today I decided to [insert your choice here] and allowed it to be mine. I did not ask for permission, I did not explain myself, and I did not seek external validation. This decision belongs to me."*

Troubleshooting

"But Some of My Results Really Are Bad"

It's easy to feel good about yourself when things are going well. But what happens when you really do fail? Maybe you lost a client because of a mistake, got bad feedback at work, or found out your health numbers are in a risky range.

When things go badly, it's easy to fall into harsh self-judgment. **But accepting what happened isn't the same as denying it, and taking responsibility doesn't mean condemning yourself.**

- **Denial says**: "*The test was unfair, the client was crazy, and the doctor doesn't know what they are talking about.*" This keeps you weak because you refuse to look at reality.
- **Global Self-Condemnation says**: "*I failed the test because I am stupid. I lost the client because I am a failure. My health is bad because I am a lazy slob.*" This paralyzes you because it turns a behavioral problem into an identity defect.
- **Responsibility says**: "*My current result is poor. I made these specific mistakes, and this is the consequence. This result is valuable,*

objective data. It tells me exactly where my current skill level ends. Because my worth is not on the line, I can look at this data clearly, learn from it, and adjust my strategy for the next attempt."

A bad result is just feedback about your current approach, preparation, or skills. It doesn't say anything about your ability to grow, and it doesn't take away your right to handle the problem with dignity.

"Isn't This Just Lowering My Standards?"

Many men worry that if they stop being hard on themselves, they'll lose their drive. They think that being tough on themselves is the only way to stay disciplined, and that if they give themselves respect before reaching their goals, they'll become lazy or lose their ambition.

But this isn't how motivation really works. There's a big difference between having high standards for your actions and demanding perfect results before you let yourself feel any respect.

- **Metric**:
  The Performance Treadmill (Outsourced Worth)
  The Practice of Self-Trust (Intrinsic Worth)

- **Primary Motivator**:
  Fear of inadequacy, shame, and social rejection.
  Self-respect, curiosity, and alignment with values.

- **Response to Failure**:
  Collapse, avoidance, defensiveness, or depression.
  Analysis of strategy, course correction, and immediate retry.

- **Standards of Behavior**:
  Rigid, perfectionistic, and dependent on being noticed.
  High, consistent, and practiced even when no one is watching.

- **View of Self-Respect**:

A prize to be earned at the end of a race.
The starting ground that makes running the race possible.

When you base your self-respect on your actions instead of your results, your standards actually rise. A man who respects himself doesn't treat his body badly or let his mind go numb. He keeps up good habits and works hard, not to earn the right to exist, but because he already values himself and wants to live well.

Chapter 1 Checklist

Before moving on to the next part of your 30-day plan, make sure you have completed these steps for Chapter 1:

1. **Physical Discipline**: Cut out processed foods, stick to a regular sleep schedule, and exercise every day.
2. **Mental Fortitude**: Swap passive screen time for activities like learning, reading, or building new skills.
3. **Professional Standards**: Tidy up your workspace, follow a set daily routine, and focus fully on your tasks.
4. **Self-Respect**: Keep up with daily grooming and avoid habits that hold you back.

***

☐ **Identified Outsourced Worth**: After finishing the Day 1 exercise, write down the top three outside factors that affect your self-respect.
☐ **Separated One Event From a Verdict**: After the Day 2 worksheet, break down at least one tough situation into facts,

feelings, and what really happened.

☐ **Made One Choice Without Permission**: For Day 3, make a confident decision on your own, without asking for approval or validation.

☐ **Recorded Behavioral Proof**: Write your Proof Statement in your journal to show you followed through.

☐ **Identified Primary Controlling External Score**: Name the main way you compare yourself to others (like money, looks, dating, or status) that most affects your self-trust.

Chapter Two

Stop Rejecting Yourself First

Narrative Opening

Ethan Brooks stands near the entrance as a local meetup group gathers. The room is full of conversation, laughter, and clinking glasses. Before he approaches anyone, his mind races through worst-case scenarios: he imagines stumbling over his introduction, the group going silent, and everyone ignoring him. His heart pounds, his shoulders tense, and his breathing quickens. The imagined scene feels so real and draining that he decides to leave. He turns around, heads for the exit, and drives home before anyone greets him.

Marcus Reed sits at his desk, looking at an email from an important client. The message offers minor, constructive feedback on a report he sent yesterday. The client wants a few formatting changes and an update to one section of data. Instead of making the quick edits, Marcus starts thinking about every mistake he has made in his career. He remembers bad deals, late deliveries, and every criticism from the past ten years. Soon, a simple request feels like proof that he is falling behind and losing his edge at work.

Both Ethan and Marcus fall into a harmful pattern: they reject themselves before anyone else can. Ethan leaves to avoid a failure he only imagined, while Marcus treats small feedback as proof of total failure. In both cases, they judge themselves first, choosing the comfort of self-sabotage over the risk of real connection.

The Inner Prosecutor

To effectively challenge your inner prosecutor, learn to distinguish between constructive self-criticism that promotes growth and destructive self-sabotage that harms confidence. Recognizing this difference helps you respond appropriately and build healthier self-talk.

The inner prosecutor uses certain predictable thinking errors:

- **Cherry-picking negative evidence**: It ignores your years of good work and positive relationships, focusing only on your mistakes and awkward moments.

- **Assuming bad motives**: If you make a mistake, it says you did it because you are lazy or flawed. If you feel nervous, it calls you a coward.

- **Exaggerating consequences**: It turns small setbacks into disasters. A slow reply to a text means a friendship is ending; a small work error means you might get fired.

- **Turning uncertainty into negative certainty**: When you don't know what will happen, it fills in the worst possible outcome and treats it as fact.

- **Attacking character instead of behavior**: It jumps from "*You made a mistake*" to "*You are incompetent.*"

- **Claiming cruelty is needed for self-improvement**: It tells you that being hard on yourself is the only way to get better, making self-criticism seem like discipline.

You can spot your inner prosecutor by its common, repeated phrases. When you hear statements like 'You always ruin things,' Practice questioning their truth or replacing them with supportive thoughts like 'I am learning and improving.' This empowers you to challenge negative self-talk actively.

If you let these statements go unchallenged, you start to believe this harsh, unfair voice is telling the truth. To counter this, practice replacing self-attack with supportive self-talk, such as 'I made a mistake, but I am capable of learning from it.' This helps you develop a more compassionate inner dialogue and build confidence.

Why Self-Attack Feels Protective

It's easy to think self-criticism is just a bad habit, but it goes deeper. Your mind uses self-attack as a way to protect you from the pain of the outside world. Once you understand why self-attack feels helpful, you can start to break its hold on you.

There are several short-term, hidden benefits to self-attack:

- **Avoiding the Sting of External Rejection**: If you reject yourself first, no one else can surprise you with their rejection. By telling yourself you are too out of shape to go to the gym, too inexperienced for the job, or too boring to date, you stay home. You choose the predictable, self-inflicted pain of loneliness over the unpredictable, external pain of being turned down by someone else.

- **Lowering Expectations**: When you declare yourself a failure or a lost cause, you immediately lower the bar. If you are "incapable" of succeeding, then you don't have to put in the hard, uncomfortable effort of trying. It shields you from the responsibility of your own potential.

- **Avoiding Disappointment**: If you convince yourself that things will never work out, you never have to experience the pain of hoping for an outcome and watching it fall through. You protect yourself by living in a state of permanent, low-level defeat.

- **The Illusion of Control**: It is deeply uncomfortable to accept that you cannot control how other people react to you, whether a client will hire you, or whether a partner will stay with you. Self-attack gives you a false sense of control. If a situation goes wrong and you say, "*It's because I am fundamentally broken*," you create a simple, cause-and-effect explanation. Your mind prefers a harsh, self-inflicted explanation over the vulnerable reality of living in an unpredictable world.

- **Shame as a Crude Motivator**: Many men use self-shaming as a psychological whip to force themselves to get out of bed, go to work, or go to the gym. They believe that if they stop calling themselves lazy or weak, they will lose all momentum and spend their lives doing nothing.

This false sense of safety is actually a trap you build for yourself. Each time you reject yourself to avoid risk, you teach your mind that you can't handle life. In the end, you trade a short moment of discomfort for the lasting damage of letting yourself down.

Day 4: Catch the Charge

Today, your goal is to step back and notice your inner prosecutor. You can't change a habit you don't see, so pay attention to the negative thoughts your mind brings up and write them down.

Five-Minute Practice

Sit with a piece of paper or a notebook. Recall a moment today or yesterday when you felt a sudden drop in your mood, a spike in anxiety, or a sudden desire to withdraw from a task or conversation. Identify the exact thoughts that accompanied that shift.

Choose one specific self-accusation you made and write it down, word-for-word, at the top of the page. Do not clean up the language or make it sound polite. Write down the raw, harsh charge your mind generated (e.g., "*You completely messed up that phone call because you're socially inept and nobody wants to do business with you*").

Once the charge is written down, answer these four questions directly below it:

1. **What specific behavior am I accusing myself of**? (Strip away the insults. What did you actually do? Example: "*I stumbled over my opening sentence and paused for three seconds.*")

2. **What objective evidence supports this charge**? (Only list facts that would hold up in a court of law. Example: "*I did stumble on my words. The other person asked me to repeat myself once.*")

3. **What objective evidence contradicts this charge**? (Look for the facts your prosecutor ignored. Example: "*We finished the call, resolved the issue, and scheduled the next meeting. I have had five other client calls this week that went smoothly.*")

4. **Am I describing a temporary behavior or condemning my entire identity**? (Are you calling a single action bad, or are you declaring yourself a bad person? Example: "*I am using a three-second stumble on a phone call to declare my entire identity socially inept.*")

When you write down these negative thoughts and question them honestly, you weaken their power. You start to see that your inner prosecutor isn't telling the truth; it's just a worried voice trying to keep you from taking risks.

Day 5: Use Coach Language

Now that you know how to spot your inner prosecutor, it's time to replace that voice with a new one: the voice of a coach. To make that shift, you need to know what a good coach sounds like.

A bad coach yells insults and tells players they are worthless, without offering real help. A good coach doesn't ignore mistakes or pretend everything is fine. Instead, a good coach is honest, expects effort, and focuses on what you can do next to improve. They point out what went wrong and what to try next, but never attack your value as a person.

To change your self-talk, try the **Honest Coach Formula**. It has four steps:

1. Say what happened using only the facts, without judgment or exaggeration.

2. Point out what needs to improve; be honest about the mistake or skill gap.

3. Remove any insults or extreme words like "always," "never," or "idiot."

4. Pick the next small action you can take to move forward.

Example Walkthrough

The Prosecutor's Version: "*You are a complete coward for sitting in your car and driving away from that meetup. You're never going to make friends, and you're going to die alone because you can't even talk to normal people.*"

The Objective Version: "*You felt anxious and decided to leave the meetup before going inside. To build connections, you need to practice initiating conversations.*"

The Next Physical Rep: Open your phone and RSVP to one local event happening this week.

The Honest Coach Rewrite:

1. **State what happened**: *"I drove to the meetup, felt a high level of anxiety in the parking lot, and decided to drive home without entering the building."*

2. **Name what needs improvement**: *"Avoidance felt safe in the moment, but it prevents me from building connections and leaves me feeling isolated."*

3. **Remove insults/hyperbole**: *"I am not a coward; I am a person experiencing high social anxiety who made an avoidant choice today."*

4. **Choose the next physical rep**: *"My next rep is to select a smaller, lower-stakes social environment next week, and commit to standing inside the door for ten minutes before making any decision to leave."*

Action Step

Identify three recurring self-insults you regularly use when you make a mistake, experience a setback, or feel anxious. Write each one down, and use the Honest Coach Formula to rewrite them into clean, actionable coaching statements. Keep these statements in your notebook or phone, and read them when you notice your internal prosecutor starting to build a case against you.

Day 6: Retire Self-Deprecating Humor

Many men use self-deprecating humor as a social defense mechanism. They make themselves the butt of the joke before anyone else can mock them. They call themselves "lazy," "clueless," "the resident idiot," or "unattractive" in casual conversation, wrapping their deepest insecurities in a layer of laughter.

This might seem like harmless, self-aware fun, but it's actually self-sabotage. Your brain does not distinguish between a joke and a statement of fact when it comes to your core identity. Every time you make a self-deprecating joke to make others comfortable, you are reinforcing your own unworthiness. You are trading your self-respect for a polite, temporary chuckle from people who often do not even know how to respond to your self-attack.

Confidence Rep

Your mission today is to retire self-deprecating humor completely. Pay close attention to your conversations. Identify the moment you feel the urge to insult yourself for entertainment, to break the tension, or to create a false sense of humility.

When that moment arrives, interrupt the impulse. Replace the self-deprecating joke with one of the following options:

- **A neutral, matter-of-fact statement**: State your situation without wrapping it in an insult.
- **Honest humor that does not target your identity**: Joke about the absurdity of the situation, the weather, or a neutral external factor, not your worth.
- **Comfortable silence**: Let the moment pass without feeling the need to fill the space by throwing yourself under the bus.
- **A direct, simple acknowledgment**: Accept the reality of what is happening without adding a layer of shame.

Example

> **Instead of**: *"I'm an absolute idiot when it comes to computers; I'll probably manage to delete the entire database if you let me touch it."*
> **Try**: *"I'm still getting the hang of this system, so I'd appreciate it if you could walk me through the database access steps."*
> **Say**: *"I'm still learning how this software works, so I'm going to take my time to make sure I get the steps right."*

When you stop making yourself the target of jokes, you show yourself and others that your identity deserves respect. You no longer trade your self-worth for a quick laugh or social approval.

Scripts

To help you handle situations where you might fall back on self-criticism or self-deprecating jokes, use these simple, direct scripts. Don't add extra explanations or apologies. Just say them calmly and let them be.

Accepting a Compliment

When someone compliments you, your inner prosecutor may try to make you brush it off, point out your mistakes, or quickly give a compliment back.

> **Instead of saying**, *"Oh, it was nothing, I actually messed up the first part, and anyone could have done it,"*
>
> **Say**, *"Thank you. I appreciate you saying that."*

Responding to a Mistake

When you make a mistake at work or in your personal life, admit it simply without putting yourself down.

> **Instead of saying**, *"I'm so incredibly sorry, I can't believe I was that stupid, I'm just terrible at keeping track of these things,"*
>
> **Say**, *"I missed that detail. I will correct it and have the updated version to you by three o'clock."*

Acknowledging Nervousness

If you feel nervous in a social or work setting, trying to hide it can make you feel worse. You can admit how you feel without making it seem like a big problem or a weakness.

> **Instead of saying**, *"I'm sorry, I'm a total wreck right now, I'm really bad at speaking in front of people,"*
>
> **Say**, *"I'm a little nervous, but I still wanted to be here and share these ideas with you."*

Troubleshooting

"But Kindness Will Make Me Lazy"

The most common objection to abandoning self-attack is the fear of complacency. Many men believe that if they stop berating themselves, they will lose their edge, stop working hard, and spend their days sitting on the couch.

This fear comes from a misunderstanding about what really motivates people. Self-criticism and shame are not good long-term motivators. Shame might push you to act for a short time, but it also makes your goals feel painful and stressful. Over time, this leads to burnout, procrastination, and avoiding your goals. You stop trying, not because you're lazy, but because your goals now feel like a source of pain.

Self-compassionate accountability isn't about letting yourself off the hook or ignoring poor performance. It's about identifying your behavior, recognizing the real-world consequences, and choosing the next step without destroying your character.

- **Shame says**: *"You missed your workout today because you have no discipline and you'll always be out of shape."* (This paralyzes you and makes you want to avoid thinking about fitness altogether).
- **Self-Compassionate Accountability says**: *"You missed your workout today because you stayed up late and felt exhausted. The consequence is that you feel sluggish. Your next opportunity to train is tomorrow at 7:00 a.m. Set your clothes out tonight and adjust your bedtime."* (This keeps the focus entirely on action, recovery, and behavioral momentum).

Being kind to yourself doesn't make you lazy; it helps you keep going. It lets you face your mistakes without worrying that they define who you are.

"The Criticism Is True"

What happens when your inner prosecutor points to a genuine defect? What if you really did perform poorly, hurt someone's feelings, or fail to meet your professional standards?

When criticism is true, your job is to accept the real feedback but ignore the extreme, negative story your inner prosecutor adds. Learn to separate the facts from the drama.

- **The Data**: The factual, specific reality of the event. (e.g., "*I did not prepare sufficiently for the presentation, I stumbled over several key slides, and the client noticed.*")
- **The Drama**: The prosecutor's identity-level expansion of the data. (e.g., "*This means you are a fraud, you are completely incompetent, your colleagues think you are a joke, and you will never succeed in this industry.*")

Accept the facts right away; they are helpful. Use them to prepare better, study more, or build your skills. But don't buy into the drama. A bad performance means you need to change your approach or learn more. It never means you are broken or worthless.

Chapter 2 Checklist

To complete this chapter and move forward in your 30-day plan, verify that you have executed each of the following actions:

1. Identified your primary sources of performance anxiety and listed the specific triggers that disrupt your focus.
2. Reframed your past failures not as personal defects, but as objective data points to guide your future preparation.
3. Established a daily routine for skill building and strategy adjustment that prioritizes competence over emotional drama.
4. Committed to a feedback loop that separates your self-worth from your external results.

***

☐ **Identified main self-accusation**: Caught your inner prosecutor in the act, wrote down one specific charge word-for-word, and analyzed it using the four objective questions on Day 4.
☐ **Rewrote three insults as coaching statements**: Applied the Honest Coach Formula to three of your most common self-attacks, turning them into neutral, action-oriented instructions on Day 5.
☐ **Accepted a compliment without deflection**: Used the simple, clean script to accept praise without downplaying your worth, making excuses, or panic-reciprocating.
☐ **Interrupted one self-deprecating remark**: Caught yourself before making a joke at your own expense, and replaced it with a neutral statement or comfortable silence on Day 6.
☐ **Selected a next rep instead of running a trial**: When faced with a challenging or uncomfortable situation, focused entirely on choosing the next physical action instead of letting your mind run worst-case simulations of failure.

Chapter Three

Keep Small Promises and Build Self-Trust

Narrative Opening

Ethan feels stuck, so he creates an ambitious daily plan: wake up at 5:00 a.m., run 5 miles, read for an hour, apply to 10 jobs, and eat healthy. But by Tuesday, he oversleeps, gives up on the routine, and tells himself he has no discipline. Looking at his unfinished list, he feels defeated and starts to believe he cannot change his life.

Marcus spends his weekend doing errands for his ex-wife, helping his neighbor with a lawnmower, and staying late at work to help a colleague. Meanwhile, he puts off his own dentist appointments, ignores his car's check engine light, and keeps delaying his personal goals. By Sunday night, he feels exhausted, resentful, and out of touch with his own needs because he has put everyone else first.

Both Ethan and Marcus are stuck in a pattern of letting themselves down because they can't make and keep realistic promises to themselves. Ethan sets goals that are too hard to reach, while Marcus puts others' needs ahead of his own well-being. In both cases, they end up losing trust in themselves.

The Broken-Promise Cycle

To see why self-trust is often low, look at how you handle promises you make to yourself. Most ongoing self-doubt isn't about lacking talent or opportunity. It comes from breaking your own commitments again and again. Each time you don't follow through, your mind keeps score. Eventually, you stop trusting yourself.

The broken-promise cycle follows a highly predictable, destructive loop:

This cycle keeps going because many people misunderstand how real change happens. When you feel disappointed after a tough day, a breakup, or feeling stuck, it's tempting to plan a huge transformation. You make a strict routine, buy new things, and tell yourself that everything will change tomorrow.

Planning big changes is really just a way to escape uncomfortable feelings. It gives you a short burst of relief, even though you haven't done the hard work yet. Your brain gets a reward just from imagining a better version of yourself. But because these plans rely on short-term motivation instead of real habits, they fall apart as soon as you face real-life challenges like tiredness, stress, or a schedule change.

When you miss just one goal, you start judging yourself harshly. Instead of seeing it as a small scheduling problem or a sign that your plan was too hard, you take it as proof that something is wrong with you. You give up on the whole plan, avoid trying again, and wait until you feel bad enough to start another extreme plan that won't last.

To break this cycle, start with small promises you can genuinely keep, which will help your audience feel hopeful and capable of change even on tough days.

The Minimum Believable Promise

The way out of the broken-promise cycle isn't to push harder with the same approach. Instead, shrink your commitments until they fit what you can really do right now. This is called a "Minimum Believable Promise" (MBP).

An MBP is a promise meant to help you rebuild trust in yourself. It's not about being as productive as possible, burning calories, or getting quick results. It's about showing your brain that you do what you say you'll do.

For a promise to qualify as a Minimum Believable Promise, it must meet the following six criteria:

1. **Specific**: It cannot be vague. "*I will eat better*" or "*I will work on my career*" are untrackable. "*I will drink one glass of water before my morning coffee*" or "*I will open my resume document*" are highly specific.

2. **Fully Under Your Control:** like "*I will send one application,*" to help your audience feel confident and empowered in their ability to follow through.

3. **Small Enough to Complete:** even on a terrible day, which will make your audience feel safe and less anxious about failure.

4. **Meaningful Enough to Count**: While the action must be small, it must still connect directly to a larger personal value or goal. It should represent a micro-step in a direction you genuinely care about.

5. **Measurable**: There must be a clear, binary pass/fail line. At the end of the day, you must be able to answer "yes" or "no" to whether you completed the task. There is no room for "I sort of did it."

6. **Tied to a Larger Personal Value**: It should be a tiny

representation of the kind of person you want to become, tied to your core values. For example, clearing your kitchen sink is not just about cleanliness; it reflects your respect for your environment and your commitment to order, which keeps you motivated to maintain habits aligned with your identity.

By following through on these small promises, you start to build real proof that you can rely on yourself. You move from depending on bursts of motivation to trusting your actions.

Day 7: Choose One Seven-Day Promise

Today, your goal is to pick one simple promise and stick to it every day for the next week. Don't pick two or three, just one.

Concrete Examples of Minimum Believable Promises

- **Physical Health**: Walk outside for exactly ten minutes.
- **Environment**: Make your bed immediately after waking up.
- **Mental Focus**: Read exactly two pages of a non-fiction book.
- **Communication**: Send one delayed email or message that you have been putting off.
- **Sleep Hygiene**: Put your phone in a drawer or outside your bedroom overnight.
- **Physical Maintenance**: Complete five minutes of basic joint stretching.
- **Financial Awareness**: Record every dollar you spend each day in a simple list.
- **Preparation**: Lay out your clothes and pack your bag for the next

day before going to sleep.

Exercise

Fill out the template below to set your seven-day promise. Write these details clearly in a notebook or on your computer:

- **The Core Promise**: "*For the next seven days, I promise to...*" (e.g., walk for ten minutes).
- **The Minimum Version**: "*The absolute smallest version of this action I can take if I am exhausted or short on time is...*" (e.g., put on my shoes and walk to the end of the street and back).
- **The Ideal Version**: "*The standard version of this action is...*" (e.g., a ten-minute walk around the neighborhood).
- **Time and Place**: "*I will perform this action daily at...*" (e.g., 7:30 a.m. in the neighborhood).
- **Likely Obstacle**: "*The most likely obstacle to interfere with this is...*" (e.g., it might rain, or I might sleep in).
- **The Pre-Planned Response**: "*If that obstacle occurs, I will respond by...*" (e.g., walking inside the house or garage for ten minutes, or doing it immediately after work instead).

Don't start tomorrow by trying to overhaul your whole life. Start with one commitment, stick to it, and let it help you build self-trust.

Day 8: Close One Open Loop

An "open loop" is a small, unfinished task that lingers in your mind and drains your mental energy. It could be a broken drawer you haven't fixed, a doctor's appointment you haven't scheduled, a subscription you meant to cancel months ago, or an unpaid parking ticket on your counter.

Each of these tasks is small on its own, but together they create a constant, nagging sense of guilt. Every time you see something undone, your mind quietly reminds you that you're not keeping up. Over time, this pile of unfinished business wears down your confidence and takes away the energy you need for what really matters.

Action Step

Today, pick one small open loop that's been hanging around and finish it. It should take less than thirty minutes to do.

Examples of Open Loops to Close

- Schedule a dental, medical, or eye exam that is overdue.
- Pay a lingering bill or resolve an administrative dispute.
- Return a package that has been sitting by the front door.
- Clean and organize one highly neglected desk drawer or cabinet.
- Reply to a personal message or email that you have been avoiding.
- Repair a basic household item (e.g., change a lightbulb, tighten a loose hinge, oil a squeaky door).
- Cancel a recurring subscription or membership you no longer use.

Reflection

After you finish the task, take a moment to answer these questions:

1. How long did this task go unfinished?
2. How many minutes did it really take to complete?

3. How does the stress of putting it off for weeks or months compare to the effort it took to get it done?

Notice that avoiding a task takes more energy than just doing it. Finishing even one open loop gives you more mental space and shows you can take care of your surroundings.

Day 9: Practice the Clean Restart

No matter how well you plan, you'll eventually miss a day or break a promise. That's normal. What really hurts your self-esteem isn't the mistake itself, but how you react afterward.

Most people see a missed habit as proof they've failed and use it as a reason to quit the whole plan. To build real self-trust, you need to learn how to start fresh with a "clean restart."

The Restart Formula

If you miss a scheduled action, immediately state the following formula to yourself, either aloud or in writing:

> *"I missed the action. I will identify what interfered, adjust the plan if necessary, and complete the next available rep."*

CRITICAL INSTRUCTIONS:

- Return ONLY the edited version of the text above
- Do NOT include any commentary, explanations, or extra markdown formatting
- Preserve paragraph structure with double newlines between paragraphs

What NOT to Do When You Miss a Promise

1. **Do not double the next day's punishment**: If you miss a ten-minute walk, do not attempt to walk twenty minutes the next day to "make up for it." This over-corrects, increases friction, and sets you up for another failure. Return to the original minimum action.

2. **Do not wait until Monday**: Do not write off the rest of the week or weekend. Perform the next rep at the very next available opportunity, even if it is a Tuesday afternoon or a random Thursday night.

3. **Do not escalate the plan's difficulty**: Do not try to prove your worth by making the task harder to compensate for the miss. Keep the barrier to entry low.

4. **Do not declare the system broken**: A miss is simply a data point indicating that the environment, schedule, or friction level needs adjustment. It is not an identity verdict.

5. **Do not use a miss as an excuse to indulge**: Avoid the "what the hell" effect, where missing one goal leads to a total abandonment of all standards for the rest of the day or week.

A clean restart means picking up your routine again without guilt, self-criticism, or making big promises to do better.

The Promise Tracker

Use this straightforward example to track your progress. Don't use complicated apps or share your results online. Keep your tracker simple, private, and easy to use.

Day
Promise
Minimum Action
Completed? (Yes/No)
Primary Obstacle Encountered
Adjustment / Next Rep

Day 7
Read two pages
Read 2 paragraphs
Yes
Felt very tired after work
Read before checking phone in morning

Day 8
Read two pages
Read 2 paragraphs
Yes
None
Keep morning routine consistent

...

Troubleshooting

"But The Action Feels Too Small"

The most common complaint about the Minimum Believable Promise is that it feels too small. You might wonder, "*How will walking for ten minutes or reading two pages change my life? I need to do something bigger.*" But this comes from not understanding how real habits are built. The point of the

Minimum Believable Promise isn't to get huge results right away. It's to become the kind of person who shows up every day, no matter what.

The main goal is to build trust in yourself, not to burn lots of calories, make more money, or be super productive. If you can't keep a small, ten-minute promise when you're tired, you won't be able to handle a much bigger routine.

You have to earn credibility with small actions before you can take on bigger ones. When you consistently keep your MBP, you show yourself that you're reliable. Once you have that proof, making the habit bigger becomes much easier. Most self-improvement plans fail in the first two weeks because people try to do too much before building trust in themselves.

"I Need More Discipline"

When people have trouble sticking to their plans, they often blame it on not having enough willpower or discipline. They think they need to be tougher or more resilient.

But this isn't the real problem. Discipline isn't some special trait that only a few people have. It comes from having clarity, setting up your environment, having enough energy, and making things easier to start.

- **Clarity**: If you do not know exactly when, where, and how you will execute a task, you will waste valuable decision-making energy trying to figure it out in the moment.

- **Environmental Design**: If your environment makes execution difficult (e.g., keeping your phone next to your bed when you want to sleep better), you are forcing your brain to fight a constant, losing battle against temptation.

- **Friction Reduction**: The smaller and simpler the entry point of a habit, the less resistance you will feel. If your goal is to stretch, simply laying your mat out the night before removes a key layer of friction.

Stop waiting for a burst of discipline to help you. Instead, make it as easy as possible to start the habit you want, and keep your first steps very small so you can keep going.

Chapter 3 Checklist

To complete this phase of the action plan, ensure you have checked off each of the following components:

☐ **Selected one believable promise**: You have chosen exactly one Minimum Believable Promise that is specific, measurable, and fully under your control.
☐ **Completed one delayed open-loop task**: You have identified and resolved one lingering, minor administrative or household chore that was consuming mental energy.
☐ **Practiced restarting without self-attack**: If you missed a task, you used the Clean Restart formula and returned to action without self-flagellation or doubling the workload.
☐ **Scaled down an unrealistic plan**: You have actively rejected the temptation to create a massive, multi-step lifestyle overhaul, choosing instead to focus on micro-actions.
☐ **Recorded behavioral follow-through**: You have tracked your daily progress using the binary pass/fail template in the Promise Tracker.

Chapter Four

Enter Life Before You Feel Ready

Narrative Opening

Ethan Brooks waits in his car outside a board game night, feeling nervous and tense. He keeps telling himself to wait until he feels calm and confident before going in. After forty minutes, his anxiety hasn't gone away, so he drives home.

Marcus Reed is in a planning meeting with his team. He has a good idea to make a project run more smoothly, but he hesitates, worrying about how to say it just right. The conversation moves on, and he never shares his idea.

These stories highlight a common problem. Both men wait to feel confident before taking action. By waiting, they miss the chance to gain the experience that would actually help them build confidence.

The Readiness Trap

The readiness trap stems from a mistaken belief about how feelings and actions connect. You might think you need to feel confident and free of anxiety before trying something new, but waiting keeps you stuck and prevents growth.

The false, passive sequence looks like this:

Feel confident -> Take action -> Succeed

This approach doesn't work because it treats confidence as something you need before you act. If you wait to feel confident, you never take action, so you never get proof that you can handle things. This makes your anxiety stronger the next time.

The active, evidence-based sequence operates in reverse:

Take a manageable action -> Experience discomfort -> Survive and learn -> Repeat -> Develop confidence

Confidence doesn't drive action; it comes after you act. It builds up as you keep facing uncomfortable situations, feel anxious, and realize you can handle it.

To get past the readiness trap, remember that feeling uncomfortable doesn't mean you're doing something wrong. It just means you're pushing your limits. Embracing your beginner status can cultivate curiosity and patience, making growth feel more accessible.

The Discomfort Ladder

To prove to yourself that you can handle discomfort, you need a structured plan. A personal ten-step discomfort ladder provides a clear, gradual way to face challenges without feeling overwhelmed.

A discomfort ladder helps you break a tough area of your life into ten steps, from easiest to hardest. Working through each step in order can foster a sense of clarity and control, easing feelings of overwhelm.

Choose one specific area of avoidance to target. Common areas include:

- Social interaction with unfamiliar people
- Public speaking or presenting ideas
- Dating and romantic initiation
- Asking direct questions or requesting assistance
- Attending new events or joining groups
- Trying unfamiliar activities or hobbies
- Sharing creative or professional work early
- Asking for direct feedback or performance evaluations.

After you pick your focus area, build your ten-step ladder. Each step should be clear and measurable, so you know when it's done. You should control the step completely, and each one should be just a bit harder than the last.

Below is a example of a blank discomfort ladder. You will populate this with your own progressive steps.

- **Step 10 (Most Challenging)**: [Insert action here]
- **Step 9**: [Insert action here]
- **Step 8**: [Insert action here]
- **Step 7**: [Insert action here]
- **Step 6**: [Insert action here]
- **Step 5**: [Insert action here]
- **Step 4**: [Insert action here]
- **Step 3**: [Insert action here]

- **Step 2**: [Insert action here]
- **Step 1 (Least Challenging)**: [Insert action here]

For example, if your chosen area of avoidance is social interaction at professional events, your ladder might look like this:

- **Step 10**: Attend a three-hour networking event alone and initiate five separate conversations.
- **Step 9**: Ask a question in front of the audience during a Q&A session at a seminar.
- **Step 8**: Initiate a conversation with a senior executive at your company during lunch.
- **Step 7**: Join a group of three colleagues talking in the breakroom and contribute one point.
- **Step 6**: Attend a local professional meetup for forty-five minutes.
- **Step 5**: Ask a direct colleague for their feedback on a recent project during a one-on-one meeting.
- **Step 4**: Ask a transactional question of a colleague you do not know well in the hallway.
- **Step 3**: Make eye contact, smile, and say good morning to three people you pass in the office.
- **Step 2**: Ask a barista or cashier how their day is going and listen to the response.
- **Step 1**: Sit in a common area or coffee shop for thirty minutes without looking at your phone.

When you set clear steps, you take the guesswork out of "putting yourself out there." You focus on the step you're on, finish it, and then move to the next one.

Day 10: Complete a Two-Minute Social Rep

Your mission for Day 10 is to complete one minor social interaction where success is defined solely by your behavior, not by how the other person responds.

The point of this exercise is to stop worrying about how others react. If you judge your success by whether someone smiles or talks to you, you give away your self-esteem. If you judge success by your own actions, you stay in control of your progress.

Choose one of the following two-minute social reps to complete today:

1. **The Greeting Rep**: Make direct eye contact with a passerby, nod or smile, and say a clear, audible "*Good morning*" or "*Hello.*" Keep walking; do not wait for them to stop or initiate a conversation.

2. **The Curiosity Rep**: Ask a cashier, barista, or service worker a genuine, open-ended question that goes slightly beyond the transaction. For example: "*How has the rush been for you today*?" or "*What do you recommend on the menu today*?" Listen to their answer, thank them, and complete your transaction.

3. **The Internal Focus Rep**: Speak to a colleague or neighbor whom you normally avoid or pass silently. Ask them a simple question about their week before you look at your phone or find a distraction.

Action Steps

1. Select your rep from the options above.

2. Identify the location and approximate time you will perform it.

3. Execute the action exactly as described.

4. Immediately afterward, record the outcome. Focus on the raw fact: Did you say the words? If yes, the rep was a 100% success, regardless of whether the other person mumbled, smiled, or ignored you.

Day 11: Be Seen as a Beginner

Your mission for Day 11 is to engage in an activity where you are visibly inexperienced and need instruction or help.

Many people avoid new things because they don't like feeling inexperienced. They might skip a fitness class, avoid learning an instrument, or not ask for help with a tool, to protect their image. But this only holds you back. Letting yourself be seen as a beginner shows real self-respect. It means you care more about growing than pretending to be perfect.

Choose one of the following beginner reps to complete today:

1. **The Class Rep**: Attend a beginner-level class in your area (such as a martial arts class, yoga session, pottery workshop, or public speaking group). Inform the instructor before class starts: "*I have never done this before. I am completely new.*"

2. **The Instruction Rep**: Go to a gym, hardware store, or specialty shop. Find an employee and ask for direct instructions on how to use a machine, piece of equipment, or tool. Say: "*I don't know how to operate this. Could you show me the correct way*?"

3. **The Early Draft Rep**: Submit a rough, early draft of a project, report, or idea to a colleague or mentor. State clearly: "T*his is a rough first draft to make sure I am on the right track. I would*

appreciate your early feedback on the direction."

Exercise

After completing your beginner rep, answer the following questions in your workbook:

- What did being a beginner actually cost you?
- Did the people around you react with mockery, or did they offer support and guidance?
- Did the world collapse because you did not know everything?
- How does admitting you do not know something change your anxiety levels compared to trying to pretend you are an expert?

Day 12: Stay Five Minutes Longer

Your mission for Day 12 is to enter a situation that you normally escape early and commit to staying for five additional minutes without using your phone or other distractions as a protective shield.

When you feel anxious in a social setting or meeting, your first reaction might be to leave, step outside, or look at your phone to seem busy. This helps you feel better for a moment, but it also teaches you that the situation is too much for you to handle.

If you stay in the situation for five minutes after you want to leave, you give your body a chance to get used to the feeling. You show yourself that anxiety doesn't last forever; it gets strong, then fades if you stick with it.

Instructions

1. Identify a situation today that triggers a desire to escape or hide (e.g., a crowded breakroom, a social gathering, a meeting where

you do not know many people, or a busy public space).

2. Enter the situation. When you feel the urge to pull out your phone, look at the time, or leave, start a mental five-minute timer.

3. During these five minutes, keep your phone in your pocket. Stand or sit comfortably, keep your posture open, and observe your surroundings.

4. Pay close attention to your physical sensations. Notice your heart rate, your breathing, and the tight feeling in your chest. Do not fight these sensations; observe them as physiological events.

5. Observe your mind's catastrophic predictions (e.g., "*Everyone is looking at me*," "*I look stupid*," "*I need to get out of here*"). Label these thoughts as "predictions," not facts.

6. After five minutes, you can decide to leave or stay. The point isn't to suffer for hours, but to show yourself you can handle five minutes of discomfort.

Scripts

Use these plain, direct scripts to navigate common social entry points and assert your presence without performing or apologizing.

Entering a Conversation

Use this script when you want to join an ongoing conversation at a social or professional gathering.

> "*Hi, mind if I join you?*"
>
> "*I overheard you talking about [topic]. I'm interested in that. I'm [Your Name].*"

Joining a Group

Use this script when you are standing near a group and want to introduce yourself.

> *"Hi, I don't think we've met yet. I'm [Your Name]."*
>
> *"Hi everyone, I wanted to introduce myself. I'm [Your Name], and I just started in the [Department/Group]."*

Asking a Question

Use this script when you need clarification but are afraid of appearing unintelligent.

> *"I want to make sure I understand this fully. Could you explain how [specific part] works?"*
>
> *"I'm not clear on the next steps for this project. What is the immediate priority?"*

Admitting Inexperience

Use this script to state your beginner status cleanly without shame. -

> *"I'm new to this area, so I'm still learning the standard process."*
>
> *"I haven't worked with this system before. Is there a guide or resource you recommend I start with?"*

Troubleshooting

"The Interaction Was Awkward"

Feeling awkward is normal, especially when you're trying something new. It doesn't mean you're bad at socializing or that something is wrong with you. An awkward moment means two people were a little out of sync. It doesn't say anything about your worth.

If something feels awkward, don't rush to escape or talk too much to cover it up. Just notice it happened and remind yourself it's okay. Take a breath, relax, and move on. The more you accept awkward moments, the less they will bother you.

"Someone Reacted Badly"

Sometimes, even if you're polite and clear, someone might ignore you, roll their eyes, or answer sharply. When this happens, you might want to give up and think you shouldn't have tried.

You must separate your respectful behavior from the other person's reaction. You have control over your actions, your tone, and your respectfulness. You have zero control over: - The other person's current stress level or bad day

- Their personal communication style or social anxiety
- Their biases, preferences, or preoccupations
- Their level of manners or emotional maturity.

If you politely ask a cashier a question and they ignore you or respond rudely, that's about them, not you. You did your part and got your proof. Their reaction is just background noise you don't need to worry about.

Chapter 4 Checklist

To complete Chapter 4 and move to the next phase of the program, verify that you have checked off the following action items:

☐ **Created a Personal Discomfort Ladder**: I have selected one avoided area of my life and written out a clear, ten-step progressive exposure ladder with specific, measurable steps.

☐ **Completed One Micro-Social Rep**: I executed a two-minute social action (Greeting, Curiosity, or Internal Focus Rep) and defined success solely by my own behavioral follow-through.

☐ **Allowed Myself to Be Seen as a Beginner**: I engaged in one activity where I was visibly inexperienced, openly acknowledged my beginner status, and tolerated the discomfort of not being an expert.

☐ **Remained in One Uncomfortable Situation Five Minutes Longer**: I entered a challenging environment, resisted the urge to use my phone or flee when anxiety spiked, and observed my sensations for five full minutes before making a decision.

☐ **Measured Participation Over External Approval**: I recorded my daily progress based on my physical actions rather than the reactions, smiles, or validation of the people around me.

Chapter Five

Respect Your Body Without Making It Your Verdict

Narrative Opening

Ethan Brooks hasn't opened his social media in three days without feeling a heavy weight in his chest. At home, he scrolls through fitness influencers and compares his body to their carefully staged photos. These images show a level of muscle and low body fat that feels far from his own reality. When he looks in the bathroom mirror, he decides there's no point in trying to date or meet new people because of how he looks. He cancels plans to join a local sports group, convinced his appearance will keep him out of the social world.

Marcus Reed looks at his receding hairline and recent weight gain in the mirror, feeling the effects of getting older. He compares his current self to how he looked at twenty-five and feels like he's failed. Sometimes he searches for extreme fitness makeovers, like strict diets or tough workout plans, but other times he gives up on even simple healthy habits. On his worst days, he skips his morning walk and eats fast food at his desk, thinking that if he can't have a perfect, youthful body, there's no reason to care for himself at all.

Both Ethan and Marcus are caught in the same cycle where their physical traits shape their self-worth. Ethan perceives his reflection as a barrier to connection, while Marcus feels his hairline and stomach diminish his value as a man. Highlighting how they turn physical facts into harsh judgments can help readers see their own patterns of self-criticism and understand the importance of changing this mindset.

Appearance Matters, but It Is Not a Moral Score

Let's start with a clear look at reality. Your body is how you experience life. It's real, and how you present yourself does matter. However, appearance is not a moral score; it doesn't determine your value as a person. We won't pretend otherwise with empty positive sayings.

- **First impressions are real**: Human beings are hardwired to process visual data rapidly. Clean grooming, clothes that fit, and a standing posture that does not seek to minimize your height will alter how people receive you in professional and social environments.

- **Physical capability improves well-being**: Having cardiovascular stamina, functional strength, and joint mobility directly correlates with lower systemic inflammation, better mood regulation, and higher daily energy levels.

- **Attraction is a physical reality**: In the dating world, physical attraction is a real threshold. People have distinct, varying physical preferences, many of which are highly subjective and outside of your direct control.

- **Genetics and aging impose absolute limits**: Bone structure, height, hair-follicle sensitivity to hormones, metabolic baselines, and the natural passage of time are biological facts. Accepting these can help your audience feel more at peace with their reality.

Knowing these facts shouldn't make you feel hopeless. Instead, it's the first step toward trusting yourself. The real problem comes when you let these physical facts turn into judgments about your worth. Having a bad hair day, losing hair, gaining weight, or being shorter than some influencer online doesn't take away your dignity.

Taking care of your body should be about respect, not punishment. You do these things because you value your body, which can help your audience feel more empowered and compassionate toward themselves.

The Comparison Machine

Today's world has created a system that takes advantage of our insecurities about appearance to make money. To protect your self-confidence, it helps to understand how this system works.

This machine relies on several distinct components:

- **Curated Feeds**: Social media algorithms prioritize extreme visual examples, which can make you feel inadequate. Recognizing this helps your audience feel understood and less alone in their struggles.

- **Dating-App Metrics**: Digital dating platforms function on rapid visual sorting. This artificial environment compresses complex human attraction into a two-dimensional swipe, leading many men to believe that a lack of digital matches represents a universal rejection of their physical self.

- **The Upgrade Cycle**: Fitness, supplement, and grooming industries generate revenue by convincing you that your current physical state is an urgent problem requiring a financial solution. They associate their products with status, sexual dominance, and absolute happiness.

- **Confirmation Bias**: Once you believe you are physically inadequate, your brain selectively searches your environment for proof. You will notice the one highly fit man in a room of fifty people and ignore the forty-nine other ordinary men who are living productive, connected lives.

This system leads you to compare your real, everyday struggles with someone else's best moments online. You see your own tiredness, bad hair days, and casual clothes, but only see others at their best. This isn't real feedback; it's a false picture that can leave you feeling stuck, ashamed, and wanting to buy things to fix yourself.

Day 13: Conduct a Comparison Audit

Today, you'll figure out exactly what makes you doubt your body and start removing those triggers. You can't build self-confidence if you keep looking at content that's meant to make you feel less than enough.

Five-Minute Practice

Take out a sheet of paper or open a digital document. Draw five columns and label them as follows:

1. **Trigger Event**: What did I look at, watch, or read? (e.g., "*Scrolled Instagram fitness page for 15 minutes,*" "*Looked at professional style forum,*" "*Compared myself to a colleague at the gym*").

2. **Immediate Feeling**: What physical or emotional sensation arose? (e.g., "*Tightness in chest,*" "*Dull shame,*" "*Sudden urge to skip lunch*").

3. **The Silent Conclusion**: What did my mind assume about my worth? (e.g., "*I will never look like that, so women will never find me attractive,*" "*I am letting myself fall apart*").

4. **Resulting Behavior**: What did I do next? (e.g., "*Closed the*

app and sat on the couch," "Ordered high-calorie comfort food," "Withdrew from my evening plans").

5. **Mitigation Action**: What immediate boundary can I set? (e.g., *"Mute this account," "Put phone away during workouts"*).

Action Step

Identify three online sources, whether they are fitness influencers, lifestyle vloggers, or forums, that consistently trigger a sense of physical inadequacy or comparison. Use your device's settings to mute, unfollow, or block these sources immediately.

This isn't weakness or running away. It's setting a healthy boundary. You're taking back your attention and protecting yourself from messages designed to make you feel insecure.

Workbook Prompt

Use the template below to document your commitment to clean focus:

Comparison Audit Log Date: ___________________

Trigger Source 1 to Remove: _______________
Why it triggers me: _______________
Action Taken (Muted/Unfollowed/Blocked): [ ] Yes [ ] No

Trigger Source 2 to Remove: _______________
Why it triggers me: _______________
Action Taken (Muted/Unfollowed/Blocked): [ ] Yes [ ] No

Trigger Source 3 to Remove: _______________
Why it triggers me: _______________
Action Taken (Muted/Unfollowed/Blocked): [ ] Yes [ ] No

Question: What does my mind do with the extra mental space when I am not comparing my ordinary physical life to a curated online highlight reel?

Day 14: Complete a Respect-Based Appearance Upgrade

Today, you'll do something to improve how you present yourself, not to hide who you are, but to show your body the care and respect it deserves.

Confidence Rep

Choose one of the following practical actions to execute today. Select the one that has been most neglected:

1. **The Grooming Action**: Schedule a professional haircut, trim your beard with precision, or invest in basic, fragrance-free skin care (cleanser and moisturizer) and apply it today.

2. **The Fit Action**: Go through your wardrobe and select one outfit that fits your current body size perfectly. If your clothes are too baggy or too tight because you are waiting to reach a "target weight," put them aside. Wear clothes that fit your actual dimensions today. Clean, iron, or steam them.

3. **The Maintenance Action**: Thoroughly clean and polish your primary pair of daily shoes. Replace worn-out laces.

4. **The Nourishment Action**: Prep a single, balanced meal containing whole foods, lean protein, and vegetables. Eat it slowly at a clean table without looking at a screen.

Key Question

While you do this, ask yourself:

> *"Am I doing this because I respect myself and want to care for my vehicle, or am I doing this out of panic, trying to run away from the body I currently have?"*

If you start to feel anxious, pause. Take a deep breath and remind yourself that your body deserves care right now. Finish the task as a simple act of self-respect.

Day 15: Practice Neutral Body Language

Today, you'll practice describing your body without harsh or dramatic self-criticism. Instead, you'll focus on the facts and take positive, respectful steps forward.

Example Walkthrough

Study how to translate emotionally charged self-attacks into neutral, objective assessments:

- **Emotional Verdict**: *"I look disgusting and fat in this shirt. I've completely let myself go, and I'm a slob."*
- **Fact-Based Neutral Translation**: *"My current weight is fifteen pounds higher than my preferred baseline. This shirt is tight around my midsection."*
- **Controllable Element**: *"I can choose the nutritional content of my next meal and walk for twenty minutes today."*
- **Acceptance Element**: "I cannot lose fifteen pounds in twenty-four hours, and carrying extra weight does not diminish my intelligence, reliability, or character."
- **Respect-Based Action**: *"I will wear a shirt that fits comfortably*

today and track my meals in a log."

Worksheet

Complete the template below for three specific physical attributes you regularly criticize.

Physical Attribute 1: ____________________

- **Emotional Verdict (What my inner critic says):** ____________________
- **Fact-Based Neutral Translation (The objective reality):** ____________________
- **What can be influenced?** ____________________
- **What must be accepted?** ____________________
- **Action reflecting self-respect today:** ____________________

Physical Attribute 2: ____________________

- **Emotional Verdict (What my inner critic says):** ____________________
- **Fact-Based Neutral Translation (The objective reality):** ____________________
- **What can be influenced?** ____________________
- **What must be accepted?** ____________________
- **Action reflecting self-respect today:** ____________________

Physical Attribute 3: ____________________

- **Emotional Verdict (What my inner critic says): ____________________**
- **Fact-Based Neutral Translation (The objective reality): ____________________**
- **What can be influenced? ____________________**
- **What must be accepted? ____________________**
- **Action reflecting self-respect today: ____________________**

Troubleshooting

"But Dating Really Is Harder for Me"

Let's be honest: it might be harder. If you're shorter than average, losing hair early, or going through big physical changes, some parts of the dating world may be less open to you. Some people care a lot about looks, and dating apps often reduce people to quick visual choices. Pretending this isn't true isn't helpful.

But knowing things are tough doesn't mean you should give up. Here's how to handle this reality without losing hope:

- **Control your presentation**: You cannot change your height, but you can control your grooming, the fit of your clothes, your posture, and your personal hygiene. Maximizing what you can control is an act of self-respect.
- **Diversify your exposure**: Dating apps are not the total of human interaction. They are a highly specific, visually dominant medium. Real-world social settings, such as interest groups,

classes, volunteer projects, and community gatherings, allow people to experience your voice, humor, reliability, and presence alongside your physical form.

- **Build a life, not a resume for selection**: If your entire existence is structured around trying to make yourself appealing to a hypothetical partner, you will project a palpable, desperate neediness. Focus on building skills, maintaining deep friendships, and engaging in hobbies that interest you. A man who is actively engaged in a meaningful life is fundamentally more attractive than a man who is waiting to be saved by a relationship.

"Fitness Is the Only Thing That Makes Me Feel Good"

Exercise is great for managing stress and staying healthy, but making your looks or strength the only thing you value about yourself is risky.

If your confidence depends entirely on your ability to lift a specific weight, run a certain pace, or maintain a precise body composition, you remain highly vulnerable to:

- **Injuries**: A torn muscle, a joint issue, or a back injury can instantly halt your training, leaving you without your primary coping mechanism and causing your self-esteem to plummet.

- **Illness**: Periods of physical illness that require rest will feel like moral failures rather than natural biological processes.

- **Natural Aging**: Your body will change over time. Metabolic rates shift, recovery times lengthen, and peak physical outputs naturally decline. If you fight this reality with anger, you will spend the second half of your life in a state of permanent mourning for your past self.

Real self-confidence comes from caring for your body and also building other parts of who you are, like your reliability, boundaries, interests, creativity, and how you support others. Your body is your home, but it's not all that you are.

Chapter 5 Checklist

Review your progress over the last three days. Place a checkmark next to each completed task once you have accumulated the necessary behavioral proof:

☐ **Identified strongest comparison trigger**: You have pinpointed the exact digital platform, account, or physical environment that most frequently prompts you to compare your appearance to others.
☐ **Reduced exposure to three trigger sources**: You have actively muted, unfollowed, or blocked three online sources of physical comparison to protect your attention.
☐ **Completed one respect-based appearance action**: You have performed a concrete task, such as a haircut, a clothing fit adjustment, shoe maintenance, or a nourishing meal, to care for your physical self today.
☐ **Described my body using neutral, non-insulting terms**: You have completed the Fact-Based Neutral Translation worksheet, separating physical realities from emotional verdicts.
☐ **Separated controllable physical improvements from intrinsic worth**: You have identified what you can actively influence regarding your health and appearance, while practicing acceptance for biological and genetic limits.

Chapter Six

Say What You Mean and Set Boundaries

Narrative Opening

During a casual lunch with his department, Ethan Brooks stays quiet while his coworkers discuss a heated political topic. He actually disagrees, based on his own reading and experience. When a colleague asks, "*What do you think, Ethan? You agree, right*?" Ethan feels anxious. Instead of sharing his view or politely opting out, he smiles, nods, and says, "*Yeah, absolutely, that makes a lot of sense*." Later, he feels empty and frustrated with himself, knowing he sacrificed honesty for comfort. This highlights the need to express your true thoughts to set healthy boundaries and communicate needs effectively.

At the same time, Marcus Reed gets a text from his ex-wife on Friday night. She asks him to take over her weekend pet-sitting at the last minute because her plans changed. Marcus had already planned a rare trip to see his brother, whom he hasn't seen in six months. Feeling tense, he quickly replies, "*Sure, no problem, I can handle that*." He cancels his trip, makes up an excuse to his brother, and spends the weekend alone and frustrated. As he takes care of the pets, he complains to himself that his boundaries are ignored, forgetting that he allowed his own plans to be pushed aside.

Ethan and Marcus both fall into the same pattern. They believe that keeping others comfortable is the only way to feel safe or valued. By always taking the easy way out, they end up ignoring their own needs. They hope being agreeable will earn respect, but instead, they build up resentment and teach others to overlook their limits and preferences.

The People-Pleasing Contract

Every people-pleasing habit is based on an unspoken, one-sided deal. This is called the People-Pleasing Contract. It's an unconscious agreement you make with others, built on a simple but flawed idea:

"I will suppress my own needs, hide my true opinions, and manage your emotional comfort at all costs so that you will never be upset with me. In return, you must validate my worth, love me, and never abandon or criticize me." The tragedy of this contract is that the other person has no idea they have signed it, which undermines your boundaries and self-respect, leaving you to pay the price for a deal they never agreed to.

This contract isn't about real kindness. It's about wanting control and safety. When you follow this contract, you aren't giving freely. Instead, you use agreement to avoid conflict and to try to get approval from others.

This contract always fails. First, the other person doesn't know it exists. They see that you are easygoing and rarely say no, so they keep asking for your help and agreement. Second, because you hide your real thoughts to avoid conflict, your relationships become weak. If people only like you because you never disagree, they don't really know you; they like the version of you that goes along with everything.

This unspoken contract leads to strong resentment. You start to feel bitter when others ask things of you, even though you agreed to help. You wish they could guess your needs, even though you never share them. Over time, this resentment shows up as passive-aggressive remarks, pulling away, putting things off, or sudden anger over small issues. To stop this cycle, you need to see that the contract isn't real. You can't control what others think of you by giving up who you are.

Kindness Versus Appeasement

Many men avoid setting boundaries because they think it means being selfish or unfriendly. They believe being a good friend, partner, or coworker means always saying yes. To build real self-esteem, you need to tell the difference between true kindness and saying yes out of fear.

Kindness

Kindness is a generous choice you make freely. It comes from feeling strong and having enough to give. When you are kind, you truly want to help and have the energy and resources to do it without hurting yourself. You don't expect anything in return, not praise or repayment. Because it's honest, kindness doesn't lead to resentment.

Appeasement

Appeasement is a reaction based on fear. It means giving in to what others want to avoid conflict or rejection. When you appease, you hide your real thoughts because you think speaking up will cause problems you can't handle. This approach wears you out over time. It also teaches others to ignore your limits and makes your relationships feel one-sided, where you are always the one taking on everyone else's discomfort.

Boundaries Are Information

To set healthy boundaries, you need to let go of common myths about them. Boundaries are not weapons or threats. They are not meant to punish, control, or change someone else. If you set a boundary to make someone act differently, that's not a real boundary; it's manipulation.

A healthy boundary is just clear information. It means stating your limits, what you can accept, what you will do, and what will happen if those limits are crossed.

A boundary is like a property line or a stop sign. The sign doesn't yell or insult drivers; it just shows the rule and where to stop. When you share a boundary, you help others know how to interact with you. This way, they don't have to guess your limits, which is respectful to both of you. Clear boundaries foster mutual respect and understanding.

For example:

- **Not a boundary (Control attempt)**: *"You need to stop raising your voice at me right now."*
- **A real boundary (Self-directed)**: *"I will not participate in a conversation where voices are raised. If you continue to yell, I am going to hang up the phone, and we can try talking again tomorrow."*

This shows boundaries as clear limits, not control or punishment, helping others understand your limits without guessing.

In this approach, your boundary doesn't depend on the other person changing right away. If they keep yelling, you follow through and hang up. You don't argue, debate, or wait for their approval. You do what you said to protect your peace.

Day 16: State One Preference

Your mission on Day 16 is to practice stating a simple, clear preference in a low-stakes environment without over-explaining, apologizing, or minimizing your choice.

Many men often say things like *"I don't care," "Whatever you want,"* or *"Anything is fine,"* even when they have a real preference. This small habit makes you disappear a little each time. By not saying what you want, you avoid the small risk of disagreement, but you also lose some control over your life. Today, you'll practice speaking up and sharing your choice.

Five-Minute Practice: Preference Drills

Take five minutes to practice saying your preferences out loud in an empty room or write them in your journal. Notice how it feels to make a direct statement without adding words like "sorry," "if that's okay," or "it doesn't really matter."

- *"I prefer Saturday morning for our meeting."*
- *"I would rather eat somewhere quieter today."*
- *"I don't agree with that approach; I think we should try this way instead."*
- *"I'd like some time to think about this before I give you an answer."*
- *"That option doesn't work for my schedule."*

Action Step: Execute One Preference Rep

In your next interaction today, whether deciding where to go for lunch, choosing a meeting time, selecting a task to focus on, or discussing plans with a partner, state your preference clearly and directly.

1. **Identify the moment**: When someone asks for your input or when a group decision is being made, pause before you default to passive agreement.
2. **Deliver the preference**: State your choice using *"I prefer," "I would rather,"* or *"My choice is."* Keep it to one concise sentence.
3. **Stop after you state your preference**: Don't explain or defend your choice, and don't apologize for having one. Let your

statement stand on its own.

4. **Accept whatever happens next**: The group might not pick your option, and that's okay. Success today means you spoke up about what you want, not whether your choice was picked.

Workbook Prompt

Write down the exact words you used to share your preference today. How did your body feel right before and after you spoke? Did you want to take it back, apologize, or laugh to make it softer? If so, how did you deal with that feeling?

Day 17: Decline One Request

Today, your goal is to say "no" to one request, invitation, or commitment that you don't have the time, energy, or interest to do.

Appeasement grows when you're afraid to say "no." Each time you agree to something out of guilt or fear of letting someone down, you give up your time for a short burst of approval. Saying "no" clearly is key to personal freedom. It shows your mind and body that you can handle the discomfort of disappointing someone without falling apart.

The No-Script Library

Pick one of the direct, honest templates below to say no to a request today. Don't lie, make up excuses, or invent emergencies. Keep your answer short and clear.

- **The Basic No**: Use this for simple, everyday requests.
  – **Script**: *"I can't take that on right now."*
  – **Why it works**: It is highly respectful, professional, and leaves no room for debate or negotiation.

- **The Warm No**: Use this for friends, family, or colleagues you care about.
  – **Script**: *"I appreciate you asking me, but I'm not available to help with that."*
  – **Why it works**: It acknowledges the connection positively while maintaining an absolute limit on your availability.

- **The Alternative No**: Use this when you genuinely want to assist but cannot meet the specific parameters of the original request.
  – **Script**: *"I can't do Friday night, but I could stop by for an hour on Sunday morning to help."*
  – **Why it works**: It establishes a clear, self-directed boundary while still offering a constructive, realistic alternative on your own terms.

Action Step: Say No to One Request

Look for a request today, maybe an event you don't want to go to, extra work you can't handle, or a favor that doesn't fit your priorities, and say no using one of the scripts above. If nothing comes up today, think of a past request you've been avoiding and send your "no" by message or email.

Workbook Prompt

Think about what you expected to happen when you said "no" and what really happened. Did the other person get upset, or did they accept it? How much mental energy did you save by saying no right away instead of putting it off or doing it with resentment?

Day 18: Communicate One Need

Today, your task is to share a personal need with someone else using a clear, step-by-step formula.

Many men stay silent, hoping their partners or coworkers will know what they need. When others can't read their minds, they feel ignored and upset. Speaking up about your needs isn't weak or needy; it's a basic part of being an adult. You have to stand up for your own well-being.

The Honest Needs Formula

To share a need without blaming or hinting, use this clear four-step process:

1. "***When [specific, observable behavior happens]...***" (State only the facts; do not assume motives or call names).

2. "***I feel [specific emotional state]...***" (Use simple feeling words like hurt, anxious, overwhelmed, or disconnected. Avoid "I feel like you," which is an accusation, not a feeling).

3. "***Because [the impact of the behavior]...***"

4. "***I need/request [specific, actionable change]...***" (State exactly what you want the other person to do, expressed in positive action terms rather than telling them what to stop doing).

Example Walkthroughs

- **Example 1: Relationship/Home**
  – **Ineffective style**: "*You always leave your clutter everywhere and expect me to clean it up. You don't respect my time at all.*"
  – **The Formula style**: "*When plans are changed at the last minute without warning, I feel anxious because I struggle to adjust my schedule. I request that we agree on our weekend plans by Thursday night whenever possible.*"

- **Example 2: Workplace**
  – **Ineffective style**: "*My boss is completely taking advantage of me and dumping all his work on my desk.*"

– **The Formula style**: "*When I receive new project tasks after 5:00 p.m. that are due the next morning, I feel overwhelmed because I cannot complete them to my standards without skipping sleep. I need us to establish a review process where tasks are assigned with at least twenty-four hours of lead time.*"

Action Step: Deliver Your Need Statement

Pick one area of tension in your life right now, with a partner, roommate, family member, or coworker. Write your statement using the Honest Needs Formula. Check that it doesn't include any insults or exaggeration. Then share it with the person in a calm, neutral way.

Troubleshooting

Boundary Guilt

When you start setting boundaries and saying "no" after years of people-pleasing, you might feel a strong wave of guilt and anxiety. Your mind may tell you that you're being selfish, mean, or hurting your relationships.

This guilt doesn't mean you've done something wrong. It's just a normal reaction when you break old habits of always saying yes. Your body is used to the false safety of going along with others, so changing that feels risky at first.

When you feel this guilt, don't try to fix it by apologizing or changing your mind. Sit with the discomfort. Remind yourself: "I'm feeling guilty because I'm learning something new, not because I've hurt anyone. This feeling will pass, and my boundary stays." With time, your mind will learn that you can handle saying no, and the guilt will fade.

Anger From Others

Some people may get frustrated, angry, or push back when you start setting boundaries. This is normal. People who were used to you having no boundaries might feel bothered when you start setting limits.

Look at this pushback calmly. Is it just them getting used to your new behavior, or does it show they only valued you when you always said yes? If someone keeps punishing, shaming, or guilt-tripping you for setting clear, respectful limits, it's a sign they don't respect your independence. Use their reaction to help you decide how close you want to be with them in the future.

Overcorrection

When men first see how much they've given up by people-pleasing, they sometimes swing to the other extreme. They go from being passive and quiet to acting hostile or aggressive. They might use boundaries as an excuse to give orders, make threats, start arguments, or treat others harshly while calling it "being honest."

This isn't real strength; it's just another kind of insecurity. True strength is calm and doesn't need to be loud. A confident man doesn't have to control or put others down to protect his boundaries. He states his limits clearly, politely, and firmly, then lets his actions show he means it. If you notice yourself enjoying shutting others down or using boundaries to punish, stop and remember: boundaries are for managing your own actions, not controlling others.

Chapter 6 Checklist

To finish Chapter 6 and make sure you've made progress, check that you've done each task below. Don't start the next chapter until you've completed everything on this list:

☐ **Stated one preference directly**: Spoke or wrote a clear preference in a decision-making moment today without apologizing, backtracking, or offering a defensive explanation.

☐ **Declined one request using a clean script**: Said "no" to an optional commitment or favor using a direct, non-manipulative script from the No-Script Library, resisting the urge to invent a fake excuse.

☐ **Communicated one personal need**: Formulated and delivered a structured statement using the Honest Needs Formula to address a specific area of friction in a personal or professional relationship.

☐ **Tolerated boundary guilt without reversing the decision**: Experienced the physical discomfort of saying "no" or setting a limit, and allowed the feeling to exist without rushing to fix it, apologize, or change your mind.

☐ **Distinguished kindness from appeasement**: Identified at least one recurring behavior in your daily life that you previously classified as "being nice" but now recognize as fear-based appeasement designed to avoid conflict.

Chapter Seven

Handle Rejection, Criticism, and Failure Without Collapsing

Narrative Opening

Ethan Brooks waits by the counter at his local coffee shop, holding his espresso. For three weeks, he has noticed a regular customer who reads design journals by the window. Today, he gathers his courage, walks over, smiles, and asks if she would like to get a drink or coffee together sometime. She looks up, smiles briefly, and replies, "That's really nice of you, but I'm actually seeing someone." Ethan feels a rush of embarrassment. He says, "No problem, have a good day," and leaves the shop. By the time he gets to his car, his thoughts are spinning. He deletes his social and meetup apps and tells himself he was foolish to try. He decides he is not meant for dating, that something must be wrong with his appearance, and that he should avoid future embarrassment by keeping to himself.

Marcus Reed sits in his office, looking at an email. He spent the last two weeks preparing a detailed consulting proposal for a local logistics business, hoping to land a long-term contract. The reply is polite but clear: "Marcus, thank you for the thorough proposal. While we appreciate your expertise, we do not have the budget for this initiative at this fiscal year's close, so we will have to pass." Marcus slowly closes his laptop. That evening, he drives home feeling sure that his skills are outdated, that his industry has moved on, and that his consulting career is over. He starts to think about quitting, seeing this one rejection as proof that he is no longer capable.

The Pain–Story–Spiral Sequence

To build real self-trust, it helps to see how one disappointing event can turn into a full-blown identity crisis. Recognizing the Pain-Story-Spiral Sequence and learning to interrupt it can inspire hope and motivate your audience to develop resilience, preventing setbacks from defining them.

This sequence has five clear stages.

1. **Trigger (Pain)**: something specific happens, like a rejected proposal, a missed goal, or a critical comment. This stage is just the initial sting of disappointment and is based on facts.

2. **Narrative (Story)**: Your mind tries to explain the pain by creating a story. Instead of seeing the event as a one-time problem, you start to believe it says something permanent about your abilities.

3. **Generalization (Spiral)**: The story grows. You link this one event to past failures and start thinking, "*I always mess things up*" or "*I will never succeed at this.*"

4. **Identity Shift**: The general belief becomes part of how you see yourself. You stop thinking, "*I failed at this task,*" and start believing, "*I am a failure.*"

5. **Paralysis**: Stuck in this new identity, you feel self-doubt and anxiety. This keeps you from taking new risks and makes the cycle even harder to break.

***

1. **A Painful Event Occurs**: You experience an objective setback. This might be a romantic rejection, a declined business proposal, a critical comment from a manager, or a failed fitness milestone. There is a natural, unavoidable sting of disappointment or hurt.

2. **The Mind Constructs a Global, Catastrophic Story**: Instead of leaving the event as a localized fact, your mind immediately begins drafting a narrative. It seeks to answer why this happened, almost always concluding that it is due to a fundamental, unfixable flaw in your character, appearance, or competence.

3. **The Body Reacts Emotionally to That Story**: Your nervous system cannot distinguish between a real physical threat and the catastrophic story you have just narrated. It responds to the story of being "fundamentally unlovable" or "professionally obsolete" with deep shame, anxiety, or heavy discouragement.

4. **You Withdraw, Isolate, or Lash Out**: To protect yourself from feeling this intensified emotional pain, you take defensive action. You delete your profiles, stop replying to messages, cancel upcoming plans, or aggressively blame external forces.

5. **Avoidance Prevents Future Corrective, Positive Experiences**: By withdrawing from the arena, you guarantee that you will not gather any new, positive evidence to disprove the negative story. The story remains unchallenged, cementing itself as an established "truth" in your mind, and your world shrinks.

If you let the Pain-Story-Spiral keep going, you start relying on others for your self-worth. When you do not get their approval, you shut down. To stop this cycle, you need to catch it at Stage Two and separate the real pain from the story your mind creates. This encourages hope and a sense of control over emotional reactions.

Rejection Is Specific

The main mistake people make after a setback is seeing rejection as a judgment on their whole worth, instead of a specific event. Understanding that rejection is just a particular incident can help your audience feel more empowered and less overwhelmed by setbacks.

To dismantle the power of any rejection, you must ask yourself objective, diagnostic questions. By stripping away emotional assumptions and focusing on what was specifically rejected, you can gain clarity and respond more effectively, building resilience against future setbacks.

- **Who rejected what, specifically**? Did a person reject your entire identity, or did they decline a specific invitation? Did a business client reject you as a human being, or did they decline a specific service proposal due to their current internal budget constraints?

- **Under what circumstances did this occur**? Was the timing poor? Was the other person dealing with personal stress, professional overload, or prior commitments that have absolutely nothing to do with you?

- **What facts are actually known**? What did the person actually say or do? Write down only what could be captured by a video camera and microphone.

- **What is completely unknown**? What assumptions are you making about their thoughts, motives, feelings, or secret judgments? Challenge yourself to answer these questions now, so you can see rejection more clearly and respond more effectively.

- **What does this event *not* prove**? Does this single event prove that you will never find a partner, never secure a client, or never improve your skills?

By answering these questions, you force your brain to distinguish clearly between four common variables that influence negative outcomes:

- **Incompatibility**: Two people or entities do not align in their current goals, values, or preferences. This is a neutral structural reality, not a personal failure.
- **Poor Timing**: An offer, invitation, or idea was presented at a moment when the recipient was unable or unready to receive it.
- **Lack of Skill**: Your current execution fell short of the required standard. This is actionable information indicating where you need to practice, not a permanent sentence of incompetence.
- **Systematic Bias or External Factors**: Factors completely outside your control, such as company restructuring, pre-existing personal relationships, or financial limitations, determined the outcome.

When you look at rejection this way, it cannot ruin your self-esteem. It stops being an emotional judgment and becomes what it really is: specific, useful information.

Day 19: Use the 24-Hour Recovery Protocol

When you face a big setback or rejection, your first job is to calm yourself and stop the Pain-Story-Spiral from starting. The 24-Hour Recovery Protocol is a step-by-step plan to help you avoid acting on impulse, stay grounded, and keep moving forward.

Step One: Stabilize (Hours 0 to 4)

Your first goal is to keep your emotions from getting out of control. Do not send quick texts, emails, or calls to explain or argue. If you need to, put your phone away. Take care of your body: eat a good meal, drink water, and get enough sleep. Being tired makes emotions worse. Move your body a little, take a walk or do a simple workout to help clear stress. Do not make any decisions about your worth, future, or abilities for the next day.

Step Two: Describe (Hours 4 to 12)

After your emotions settle, take a piece of paper and write down what happened. Keep it to five sentences or less. Use only objective words. For example, instead of saying, "*I completely blew the presentation, and everyone thought I was an idiot,*" write, "*I forgot to present slide five, and my manager asked two clarifying questions about the budget. I felt anxious during the Q&A.*" Leave out any negative labels and just describe what you and others did.

Step Three: Learn (Hours 12 to 18)

Find the practical lesson in the setback and let go of the emotional drama. Ask yourself, "*What is one useful thing I can learn from this?*" If you forgot a slide, the lesson is to use a checklist next time. If a date said no to a second meeting, maybe you were not a match, or you could practice asking better questions. Write down this one lesson. Do not create a long list of personal flaws from one mistake.

Step Four: Re-enter (Hours 18 to 24)

Do not let yourself stay isolated. Take a small, positive action within a day of the setback to show your mind that you are still moving forward. This could be cleaning your kitchen, replying to a work email, paying a bill, or doing a workout. This small step helps you break out of feeling stuck and shows you can handle disappointment without losing control.

Day 20: Ask for One Piece of Feedback

Real self-trust does not mean pretending you have no flaws. It comes from being able to look at your weak spots without feeling ashamed. On Day 20, you will ask for helpful feedback to practice taking criticism calmly and openly.

Instructions for the Confidence Rep

1. **Select a trusted colleague, peer, mentor, or friend**. Choose someone whose judgment you respect and who has observed your performance in a specific area (e.g., your work projects, your communication style, or a shared hobby).

2. **Ask a direct, targeted question**: Reach out via email, message, or in person and ask: "I'm working on improving my skills in [specific area]. What is one specific thing I could improve or do differently next time?"

3. **Apply the Active Response Rules**: Listen or read without defending yourself. Do not offer excuses, explanations, or rationalizations. Your only job is to receive the information.

4. **Ask for a concrete example if needed**: If their feedback is vague, ask calmly: "*Could you give me an example of when that happened so I can understand it better?*"

5. **Thank them directly**: Say or write, "*Thank you for the feedback. I appreciate your honesty and will think about how to apply this.*"

6. **Evaluate privately**: Step away and decide objectively what part of the feedback is useful to apply to your future actions, and discard any parts that do not serve your progress.

By doing this, you take charge of how you handle feedback. You show yourself that criticism is not a personal attack, but a useful tool for getting better.

Day 21: Repair or Retry

After a setback or rejection, it is natural to want to hide to avoid feeling that pain again. On Day 21, you will do the opposite by taking an active step to recover. You need to get back out there and either fix a mistake or try again at what did not work before.

Selecting Your Active Recovery Action

Choose one of the following concrete actions to complete today:

- **Apologize cleanly for a mistake**: If you made an error that affected someone else, offer a direct, non-defensive apology. Use the script: "*I made a mistake when I [action]. I apologize for the impact it had, and I have [action/correction] to ensure it is handled correctly moving forward.*"

- **Correct a work error**: Identify a project, report, or task that was criticized or returned. Make the necessary corrections calmly and resubmit it without complaining or over-explaining.

- **Resubmit an application or pitch**: If a proposal or application was declined, find an alternative opportunity and submit a revised version using the feedback you gathered.

- **Attempt another social conversation**: If a recent social interaction was awkward or resulted in rejection, initiate a new, brief conversation with a different person today to reset your social momentum.

- **Return to an activity you recently slipped up on**: If you missed a habit, skipped a workout, or broke a promise to yourself, return to that exact activity today. Perform one clean repetition.

Proof Statement

After you finish your recovery action, write this Proof Statement in your journal: "*The setback did not make the next decision for me. I chose my action, faced the discomfort, and stayed on my own side.*"

Rejection Recovery Card

To make sure you can use the 24-Hour Recovery Protocol during a crisis, copy the template below onto a small card, save it on your phone, or print it. Use it as a quick reminder whenever you face a tough setback.

REJECTION RECOVERY CARD

1. What actually happened? (Write 1-3 objective sentences. No adjectives, no insults, no drama.) ______________________

2. What am I making this mean about my identity? (Identify the "Inner Prosecutor's" story so you can dismiss it.) ______________________

3. What remains true about me regardless of this outcome? (List 2-3 facts about your character, skills, or efforts.) ______________________

4. What is the single practical lesson I can extract? (What is the direct, actionable feedback here?) ______________________

5. What is my unrelated next physical rep? (A simple, productive task to complete in the next 2 hours.) ______________________

6. What action would self-respect take right now? (Choose the high-integrity choice over withdrawal or lashing out.) ______________________

Troubleshooting

"But Some of My Results Really Are Bad"

It is normal to have times when your results are not good. Maybe your sales are down, your fitness has slipped, or a relationship has ended. In these moments, pretending everything is fine does not help your self-esteem. Denying the truth only hurts your self-trust.

You must understand the difference between accepting a bad result and accepting a global identity verdict:

- **Acceptance is not approval or surrender**; it is simply acknowledging reality as it exists in the present moment. If you have a poor result, saying *"I have failed to meet my sales target this month"* is a statement of reality.

- **Responsibility is not self-condemnation**: Taking responsibility means looking at the bad result and saying, *"This is my current starting point. What decisions did I make that contributed to this, and what can I do next to correct it?"*

- **A bad result is information, not identity**: A bad result tells you that your current strategy, skill level, or execution is insufficient for the outcome you want. It does not mean you are fundamentally flawed. Treat the bad result as a diagnostic scan of your car; it tells you what needs repair, not that the car should be thrown into a scrap heap.

"Isn't This Just Lowering My Standards?"

When you stop being hard on yourself after a failure, you might worry that you are getting lazy or lowering your standards. This worry comes from the mistaken idea that being tough on yourself is needed to do well.

In reality, separating your self-worth from your results allows you to maintain exceptionally high behavioral standards:

- **Flawless external results are a delusion**: You cannot control dating app algorithms, macroeconomic shifts, or another person's mood. Demanding flawless external outcomes before you grant yourself basic respect is a recipe for permanent anxiety and eventual surrender.

- **Behavioral standards are entirely under your control**: You can demand that you prepare thoroughly for meetings, treat others with respect, communicate honestly, and show up for your workouts. These are behavioral standards.

- **True accountability requires stable self-trust**: When your self-worth is not on the line with every outcome, you can look at your mistakes with absolute honesty. You don't need to lie to yourself, blame others, or hide your errors because a mistake no longer threatens your right to exist. You can simply say, "*My execution fell short of my standards here. I will correct it.*"

Divorce, Betrayal, or Major Loss

When you go through major life events like a divorce, a serious betrayal, or losing someone close to you, simple mindset shifts and daily tasks are not enough. These situations turn your world upside down and need special care.

To get through major life crises without falling apart, you need to use some protective strategies.

- **Let yourself grieve**; grief is a normal and necessary process. Trying to rush through a big loss or act as if nothing happened will only cause more pain later. Expect to feel sad, angry, or confused.

- **Keep up basic routines to stay grounded**, like waking up at the same time, drinking water, eating healthy food, and getting outside. These habits help you stay steady when your emotions are all over the place.

- **Handle legal and practical matters directly**; do not ignore emails, court dates, or bills because you feel overwhelmed. Taking care of these things step by step keeps the crisis from getting worse. Lean on support groups or a therapist; do not try to handle everything alone.
- **Find people who have been through similar things** or talk to a professional who can help you process what happened.
- **Try not to let bitterness take over**. It is easy to become cynical after a big betrayal or loss, but this only keeps you isolated and stops you from rebuilding your life. Feel the pain, but do not let someone else's actions decide how much you can trust or connect in the future.

Chapter 7 Checklist

Review your progress over Days 19 to 21. Check off each item as you build your objective evidence of resilience:-

1. I have identified the specific narrative I created about myself or others following the betrayal.
2. I have challenged my overgeneralizations and replaced them with objective, evidence-based truths.
3. I have committed to one small, daily action that demonstrates trust in myself and my future.
4. I have recognized the difference between healthy caution and self-sabotaging isolation.
5. I have documented at least three instances where my resilience proved stronger than my pain.

***

☐ **Implemented the 24-Hour Recovery Protocol**: Handled a setback by stabilizing your physical state, writing objective facts, extracting one lesson, and taking an unrelated micro-action.

☐ **Asked a Trusted Person for Feedback**: Asked for constructive criticism regarding a specific skill, listened without defending yourself, and thanked them.

☐ **Completed One Clean Repair or Retry**: Apologized for a mistake, corrected an error, or returned to a missed habit without over-explaining.

☐ **Separated an Objective Rejection From Personal Worth**: Used the diagnostic questions to isolate the specific variables of a negative outcome rather than accepting a global identity verdict.

☐ **Acted Before Feeling Fully Recovered**: Took a constructive action while still experiencing the lingering discomfort of a setback, to prove that your actions are independent of your emotional states.

Chapter Eight

Build Relationships Without Neediness or Performance

Narrative Opening

Ethan Brooks is on his sofa, looking at his phone. He had a great first date last night; they laughed over tacos, found out they both like independent films, and ended the night with a warm hug. Now, not even a day later, Ethan can't stop overthinking. He's already written and deleted five different texts, trying to sound interested but not too eager.

His phone is on the coffee table. Each time it lights up, his heart jumps, but it's always just a promo email or a system update. Hoping she might want to meet up, Ethan cancels his gym session to keep his evening free. He keeps replaying their conversation, second-guessing what he said and even changing his opinions in his mind. She mentioned liking modern architecture, which Ethan knows nothing about, but he pretended to be interested. Now he's thinking about buying books on the topic to keep up the act. By changing his plans, overthinking his messages, and trying to be someone he's not, Ethan is slowly losing himself to win her approval.

Marcus Reed is in his kitchen making coffee before starting his Saturday. He's recently divorced and dating again, but he's very guarded. He met someone interesting earlier in the week, but he's afraid of looking desperate or like he has too much baggage. To protect himself, Marcus acts cool and distant.

When she texted him to ask how his week was, Marcus waited six hours before replying. He wanted to seem busy and hard to impress. He hides his real schedule, lets her make all the dinner choices by saying, "I don't care, you choose," and keeps his personal life private. Marcus thinks that acting distant makes him look strong, but really, his act is just another way to avoid real connection. Like Ethan, he's hiding his true self to avoid rejection.

Neediness Is Not Having Needs

To build relationships that are resilient, honest, and satisfying, you must first understand a fundamental truth: having human needs is a natural part of authentic connection, not a sign of weakness.

As a human being, you possess neurobiological needs for connection, safety, validation, and belonging. Expressing these needs directly helps you feel more confident and genuine in your relationships.

Explain that wanting connection isn't neediness, helping readers understand healthy emotional needs versus unhealthy patterns.

When you act out of neediness, you treat your partner like they're responsible for your feelings. You watch how quickly they reply, their tone, or their mood to decide if you can feel okay. This puts too much pressure on them and ruins the natural connection between you.

Contrast this with healthy interdependence:

- **Needy Dependence**: *"I require your constant reassurance and immediate responses to prove that I am desirable and safe. If you pull back even slightly to attend to your own life, my self-worth* *collapses, and I will use pleasing behaviors or passive-aggressive withdrawal to force you to reassure me."*

- **Healthy Interdependence**: *"I value our connection and highly enjoy your reassurance, but my fundamental worth is already settled. If you are busy, distracted, or need space, I can tolerate the temporary discomfort of uncertainty without demanding that you drop everything to rescue me from my anxiety."*

When you accept that your needs are real but your feelings are your own to manage, you stop expecting others to prove your worth. Instead, you see them as real people you can connect with honestly.

Stop Performing for Selection

A lot of men treat dating like an audition, trying to show off a perfect version of themselves. Letting go of this performance helps you build self-trust and form authentic relationships.

When you act just to get picked, dating feels more like a sales pitch than a real search for compatibility. Here are some common ways men do this and how it hurts self-trust:

1. **The "Nice Guy" Persona**: If you hide your real opinions and needs to avoid conflict, you start to believe your true self isn't lovable. This leads to resentment when your needs aren't met.

2. **The Stoic Provider**: Trying to look completely tough and in control all the time keeps you from real closeness. You end up stuck, unable to show weakness or ask for help.

3. **The Chameleon**: If you keep changing your hobbies, opinions, or lifestyle to match your date, you lose track of who you really are. When you stop pretending, you might not even recognize yourself.

The Performance of Apathy

You act like you don't care, wait days to reply, keep your distance, or hold back real compliments. You do this to avoid seeming too eager. The cost: you attract people who like unavailability and miss out on those who want real, open communication.

Automatic Agreement

You hide your real tastes, opinions, or habits to match your partner. If she likes a restaurant, you say it's your favorite. If she dislikes something you enjoy, you stop doing it. The cost: your partner falls for someone who isn't real, and your hidden preferences turn into resentment.

Exaggerating Income, Status, or Experience

You talk a lot about your job, money, connections, or past adventures to make up for feeling not good enough.
The cost: you end up feeling anxious and worried that people will see you as ordinary.

Hiding Authentic Hobbies and Quirks

You keep your interest in unique hobbies, video games, certain books, or routines a secret because you're afraid of being judged.
The cost: you miss out on being liked for who you really are, and you start to believe your true self isn't good enough.

Utilizing Manipulative Dating "Hacks"

You use scripted lines, tricks, or games to try to make someone like you.
The cost: dating becomes about control, not connection, and you end up stuck in a cycle of anxiety and manipulation.

Putting the Other Person on a Pedestal

You think that if someone is attractive, successful, or popular, they have no flaws and are better than you. You see their attention as a prize and take their disapproval hard.
The cost: you can't have a balanced relationship if you always see yourself as less than your partner.

To build real confidence, stop treating dating like an audition. Your goal isn't to make someone like you; it's to be honest, see if you're truly compatible, respect each other's boundaries, and enjoy being yourselves together.

Day 22: Express Honest Interest

Your mission for Day 22 is to practice expressing clear, clean, and direct romantic or social interest without performance, games, or manipulative setups.

Showing interest with confidence means saying you appreciate someone or want to spend time with them, without apologizing, making it complicated, or needing them to say yes right away to feel good about yourself.

The Script

Use this direct template to initiate a date or suggest a meeting:

> *"I've really enjoyed talking to you, and I'd love to take you out for a drink sometime next week. How does your schedule look?"*
>
> *"I've enjoyed talking with you. Would you like to get coffee this week?"*

If you are already in contact and want to suggest a specific plan, you can adapt it:

> *"I really like our conversations. I'm planning to try that new Italian place on Thursday evening; I'd love for you to join me as my date."*

The Rules of Direct Expression

1. **Be specific**. Instead of saying, "*We should hang out sometime*," which is vague, suggest a clear activity like coffee, dinner, or a walk, and mention when, like this week or Saturday afternoon.

2. **Accept a "No" gracefully**. If someone says they're busy or not interested, take it well. Saying something like, "*No worries, I understand. Hope you have a great week*!" shows self-respect and maturity.

3. **Don't try to sell yourself**. Don't explain why they should go out with you or talk up the place. Just let your invitation speak for itself.

4. **Don't keep pushing**. If they don't reply or say something vague like, "*Maybe, I'll let you know*," don't send more messages or ask again. Let it go; their response tells you what you need to know.

5. **Don't apologize for showing interest**. Skip phrases like, "*Sorry to bother you*," or "*I know you're probably busy, but...*" It's normal and healthy to reach out to someone you like.

When you give a clear invitation, you show yourself that you can handle the risk of reaching out without hiding behind jokes, drinks, or pretending not to care.

Day 23: Maintain One Piece of Your Life

Your mission for Day 23 is to protect and prioritize one pre-existing personal commitment while dating or building a relationship.

When a new relationship begins, it's easy to drop your routines. You might skip workouts, forget your budget, cancel plans with friends, or lose sleep just to be available. Some flexibility is fine, but if you always put your life on hold for someone else, you start to lose yourself. It also tells both you and your partner that your own goals and commitments don't matter.

A healthy relationship should add to your life, not make you lose who you are.

The Confidence Rep

Identify one firm personal commitment that you scheduled for this week. It could be:

- Your Tuesday night gym session.
- Your weekly dinner or phone call with a close friend or family member.
- Your dedicated Sunday morning hobby, project, or rest period: your study, reading, or skill-acquisition time.

Protect this time on purpose. If your partner wants to meet during it, don't cancel. Calmly keep your commitment and suggest another time to meet.

The Script to Use

> *"I'd love to see you, but I have a commitment at that time that I need to keep. How about we meet on Friday evening instead?"*

You don't need to over-explain, apologize a lot, or make up excuses. Having your own plans and commitments is healthy and shows self-respect.

By doing this, you prove to yourself that your goals and routines are important. You don't have to drop everything to keep someone interested.

Day 24: Name an Insecurity Without Demanding Rescue

Your goal for Day 24 is to share a vulnerable feeling or insecurity healthily, without expecting the other person to fix it or change for you.

In relationships, men often go to two extremes: they either hide their insecurities by acting tough (like Marcus), or they put all their worries on their partner, asking for constant reassurance or control (like Ethan).

There's a better way: admit your insecurity is yours to handle, but share it honestly to build real closeness.

The Confidence Rep

Identify a genuine insecurity, worry, or anxious feeling you have experienced recently in your dating life or current relationship. Choose a calm moment, not in the middle of an argument, and state it clearly using the formula below.

The Script

> *"I noticed I've been feeling a little insecure about [insert topic, e.g., how quiet things have been between us yesterday]. I'm working on how I respond to that feeling internally, but I wanted to be honest with you about what's going on with me rather than acting distant or pretending I'm fine."*

The Contrast: Responsible Vulnerability vs. Demanding Rescue

Review the table below to understand the difference between healthy sharing and anxious dumping:

Responsible Vulnerability (Goal): *"I've been feeling a bit anxious about our schedule changes lately."*
Demanding Rescue (Avoid This): *"You need to stop going out so much because it makes me anxious."*

Responsible Vulnerability (Goal): Owns the emotion: *"This is my feeling to process, but I want to share it."*
Demanding Rescue (Avoid This): Outsources the emotion: *"Your behavior is making me feel this way; fix it."*

Responsible Vulnerability (Goal): States the truth without placing blame or demanding a specific performance.
Demanding Rescue (Avoid This): Uses guilt, pressure, or passive-aggression to force a reassuring reaction.

Responsible Vulnerability (Goal): Invites conversation, understanding, and mutual support.
Demanding Rescue (Avoid This): Triggers defensiveness, resentment, and emotional withdrawal.

When you share how you feel without making it someone else's job to fix it, you build real self-trust. You show yourself you can be imperfect and honest without losing your dignity or needing others to manage your feelings.

Additional Scripts

To help you navigate common relational friction points with calm authority, keep these clean, non-manipulative scripts in your toolkit.

Asking for Reassurance Responsibly

Use this when you genuinely want a moment of connection to settle your mind, but want to make sure you are not acting out of a demanding, needy impulse:

> *"I've had a stressful week, and I'm feeling a bit disconnected. I could use a little reassurance today, but I also know this anxious feeling is ultimately mine to work through. I just wanted to check in with you."*

Discussing Jealousy

Use this when you notice feelings of jealousy arising, allowing you to discuss the situation objectively without accusing your partner or displaying controlling behavior:

> *"I noticed some jealousy coming up for me when you were talking about your new colleague. I don't want to accuse you of anything or control your friendships, but I'd like to talk about it openly so I can process the feeling and make sure we're on the same page about our boundaries."*

Accepting Romantic Rejection

Use this when someone lets you know they do not see a romantic future with you, allowing you to walk away with your dignity completely intact:

> *"Thank you for being so clear and honest with me. I appreciate you letting me know, and I respect your decision. I wish you the very best."*

Troubleshooting

Overanalyzing Text Messages

Texting is a big source of anxiety in dating. If you catch yourself overthinking a message, try this:

1. **Is the message unclear**? If so, don't try to guess; ask directly or let it go.

2. **Waiting for a reply**? Put your phone down, do something else, and remember their response time doesn't define your worth.

3. **Writing a reply**? Write your honest first draft, edit for clarity, and send it without stressing about how it will be taken.

When you stop trying to read between the lines and focus on clear communication, you feel more at ease and set better boundaries.

1. **Does your message need a reply**? If you asked a direct question like, "*Are we still on for 7 p.m.*?" then yes. If it was just a comment or meme, no reply is needed. If not, stop texting, close the app, and focus on what's around you.

2. **Has it been a while**? If you're waiting for a yes-or-no answer

and it's been hours or a day, send one simple follow-up: "*Hey, just checking in to see if we're still on for tonight so I can plan my evening.*" If there's still no reply, assume they're not available and make other plans.

3. **Are you texting for clarity or to ease your anxiety**? Before you hit send, ask yourself if you're sharing useful info or just looking for a quick reply to feel better. If it's the second, don't send it. Sit with the discomfort; every minute you wait builds your self-trust.

Losing Yourself in a Relationship

It's easy to slip back into people-pleasing once you're in a relationship. Watch for these warning signs that you're losing yourself:

- **Dropping Friends**: You stop reaching out to your buddies, decline invitations, or let long-standing friendships drift because you are dedicating all your free time to your partner.

- **Hiding Preferences**: You consistently default to their choices for meals, movies, weekend plans, and home decor, slowly erasing your own voice from the shared space.

- **Total Calendar Availability**: You refuse to make plans of your own more than a few days in advance, keeping your calendar empty just in case your partner wants to see you.

- **Constant Reassurance-Seeking**: You frequently ask questions like, "*Are you mad at me*?", "*Are we okay*?", or "*Do you still love me*?" in response to minor shifts in their mood.

- **Tolerating Patterns of Disrespect**: You ignore broken promises, constant lateness, dismissive comments, or violations of your boundaries because you are terrified that addressing them will cause a conflict and end the relationship.

If you notice these patterns, don't beat yourself up. See it as helpful feedback. Pick one small thing, like planning a night out with a friend or sharing a preference, and do it calmly. You don't have to change everything; start taking back your own life.

Chapter 8 Checklist

To finish Chapter 8 and build self-trust in your relationships, check off these steps:

1. **Identify your pattern**: Write down one way you often give up your needs to keep the peace.
2. **Choose a small move**: Pick a simple action, like picking a restaurant or making time for a hobby, and plan it for this week.
3. **Execute calmly**: Do it without apologizing or looking for approval.
4. **Observe and record**: Notice how you felt before, during, and after, and how you handled any anxiety.
5. **Reflect**: See that your relationship survived this small boundary, proving you can stand up for yourself.

***

☐ Expressed interest or appreciation honestly: Initiated one clear, direct invitation or expressed genuine appreciation using a clean script without playing games or apologizing.
☐ Maintained an independent commitment: Protected at least one pre-existing personal schedule block (gym, hobby, or time with friends) instead of canceling it for relationship

availability.

☐ Communicated one vulnerable truth without demanding rescue: Shared an insecurity, worry, or anxious feeling responsibly, owning the emotion rather than accusing or demanding reassurance.

☐ Did not let another's response define my value: Practiced separating a text delay, a quiet mood, or a rejection from your own intrinsic worth.

☐ Practiced connection without performance: Identified at least one moment where you were tempted to perform (by pretending to agree, exaggerating status, or hiding a hobby) and chose to present your genuine self instead.

Chapter Nine

Build Competence and Purpose Without Worshipping Achievement

Narrative Opening

Ethan Brooks often sits on his couch with his laptop, looking at options for coding certifications, photography workshops, and local sports leagues. He compares requirements, reads reviews, and saves dozens of syllabi. But when it's time actually to register or pay, he hesitates. He imagines himself showing up unprepared, making mistakes, and feeling embarrassed. He convinces himself to wait until he's more prepared, has more time, or is sure he's talented enough before spending money or risking embarrassment. Because of this, his evenings pass by as he keeps putting off his goals, and his dreams stay stuck in a folder of bookmarks he never visits.

Marcus Reed sits at his kitchen table, looking at his calendar and feeling empty. For over fifteen years, his life and sense of purpose were tied to being the main provider and protector for his family. After his separation, everything changed. The house is quiet, routines are gone, and his responsibilities look different. Without his old role guiding him, Marcus feels lost and unsure of his purpose. He wonders who he is and what his work means now that the structure he relied on is gone.

Even though Ethan and Marcus have different lives, they share a similar problem: they tie their self-worth to achievements and roles. Ethan holds back because he can't stand feeling like a beginner and wants to be perfect before he starts. Marcus has based his purpose so much on one role that losing it makes him feel empty. Both are waiting for outside approval or a sure sign before they take action.

Competence Creates Evidence, but Not Worth

Learning a real, hands-on skill is one of the best ways to build genuine self-confidence. When you focus on doing, you leave behind doubts about being a genius or a failure and start seeing real results from your efforts, which can inspire a sense of empowerment.

When you work on building a skill, you build self-trust in five ways:

- **Mastery Experiences**: You see how your effort leads to real results. If you practice and notice a task gets easier, you prove to yourself that you can improve.

- **Objective Feedback**: The task itself doesn't care about your doubts. If your code has an error or your wood joint is uneven, you get honest feedback. You learn to see mistakes as problems to fix, not as personal failures.

- **Frustration Tolerance**: Learning something new means being okay with not knowing what you're doing at first. By sticking with it, even when it's hard, you show yourself you can handle frustration.

- **Visible Progress**: Unlike feelings, which change all the time, skill progress leaves a clear trail. A finished table, a working script, or a completed budget shows what you've done.

- **Pride in Effort**: You gain self-respect from the work itself, not just from perfect results or praise.

Remember that building skills helps you trust yourself, but your worth isn't tied to success. Many use achievement to hide feelings of shame, which can make you feel inadequate. Recognizing this can help the audience feel more accepted and less judged by their current state.

If you rely on achievements to feel good about yourself, you'll notice that the goalposts keep moving. A promotion or certificate might feel great for a moment, but soon you'll be chasing the next thing. This makes your confidence fragile, because any setback or change can shake your sense of self. Real self-esteem comes from knowing your value doesn't depend on achievements. You build skills to take part in life, not to prove you deserve to exist.

Purpose Is a Direction, Not a Lightning Bolt

A common myth in self-improvement is that purpose comes as a sudden, magical moment of clarity, like a lightning bolt that reveals your true calling. This idea often keeps people waiting for inspiration instead of taking action.

In truth, you don't find purpose by waiting for it. You build it gradually through small actions. Purpose is a direction you choose, where your efforts help something beyond your own comfort. Starting with small steps can create the motivation you thought you needed first.

To find traction, you do not need a grand, fifty-year blueprint. Instead, identify your current skills and values to select purpose avenues that align with what you can contribute now, making your efforts more targeted and achievable.

Consider these ten distinct avenues of purpose, none of which require you to be a flawless achiever to begin:

- **Creating:** Designing, building, writing, or assembling something tangible that did not exist before, whether it is a piece of furniture, a software program, or a garden.
- **Teaching**: Passing on clear, verified knowledge or practical skills to someone who is currently trying to learn them.
- **Protecting**: Exercising your physical, financial, or legal capability to safeguard vulnerable individuals, your family, or your local community from harm.
- **Learning**: Committing yourself to the rigorous study of a specific topic, trade, or discipline to expand your understanding and capacity.
- **Serving**: Providing reliable, necessary labor that supports the well-being, health, or safety of others without requiring personal spotlight or praise.
- **Mentoring**: Offering steady guidance, active listening, and objective support to a younger colleague or family member navigating life decisions.
- **Repairing**: Restoring order to things that are broken, whether that means fixing physical machinery, restoring neglected properties, or resolving damaged relationships.
- **Leading**: Stepping forward to organize, direct, and carry the responsibility for a group of people working toward a shared, constructive goal.
- **Building**: Constructing systems, businesses, organizations, or community groups that provide long-term utility and structure for others.

- **Caring**: Dedicating your daily attention and physical labor to supporting the health, development, and daily life of family members or animals.

When you pick just one of these paths and take a small step, you move from thinking about what you deserve to thinking about what you can give or create. This change helps you feel less anxious and more useful right away.

Day 25: Choose a Thirty-Hour Skill

Five-Minute Practice

Take out a notebook or open a blank document. Write down three real-world skills you've avoided because you were worried about looking inexperienced or wasting time. Choose skills where thirty hours of focused practice would make a real difference. For example: cooking healthy meals, public speaking, basic weightlifting, woodworking, coding a simple webpage, doing basic home repairs, or managing your budget. Pick one skill to focus on for this challenge.

Action Step

Fill out the "Thirty-Hour Skill Worksheet" to turn your goal into a real plan:

1. Write down the skill you want to learn.

2. Break it into smaller parts you can practice one at a time.

3. Decide what success looks like after thirty hours.

4. List the tools or materials you'll need.

5. Think about what might get in your way and how you'll handle it.

6. Set aside specific times in your calendar to practice until you reach thirty hours.

Thirty-Hour Skill Worksheet

1. **The Selected Skill**:
   Example: Basic Home Woodworking (specifically, building a simple, sturdy wooden bookshelf).

2. **Why This Skill Matters to Me**:
   Example: I want to be able to build and repair physical items in my living space with my own hands, moving away from relying entirely on cheap, pre-assembled furniture.

3. **My First Milestone (The 5-Hour Mark)**:
   Example: Learn how to safely operate a circular saw, make straight cuts on a 2x4 board, and successfully join two pieces of wood using pocket holes.

4. **My Weekly Practice Schedule**:
   Example: I will practice for 3 hours every week, specifically, 1 hour on Tuesday evening (technical reading/watching tutorials) and 2 hours on Saturday morning (active practice in the garage).

5. **The Beginner Embarrassment I Am Willing to Tolerate**:
   Example: I am willing to cut wood to the wrong length, make uneven cuts, ask basic questions at the hardware store, and feel clumsy holding tools for the first few sessions.

Day 26: Complete One Career or Life Move

Action Step

Think of one specific work or life task you've put off because you were overthinking, afraid of rejection, or waiting for the perfect moment. Today, take one real step that leads to an actual result instead of just planning.

Select one of the following options and complete it within the next two hours:

- **Update Your Resume**: Open your current resume and update your employment dates, add your latest concrete achievements, and format it cleanly. Export it as a PDF so it is ready to send.
- **Request a Meeting with a Manager**: Send a short, professional email to your supervisor or manager requesting a fifteen-minute meeting next week to discuss your performance, professional development, or a specific project idea.
- **Apply for a Role**: Submit an application for a professional position that matches your current qualifications, accepting that a potential rejection is useful market feedback, not an identity verdict.
- **Sign Up for a Certification**: Register and pay for a professional certification, exam, or course that is directly relevant to your field of work.
- **Organize Your Budget**: Open a spreadsheet, list your exact bank balances, outstanding debts, recurring monthly expenses, and set a simple, realistic savings target for the next thirty days.
- **Schedule a Physical**: Call a local medical clinic and schedule an annual physical exam or dental check-up, closing a health-related open loop that has been causing silent worry.

Day 27: Write a Contribution Statement

Five-Minute Practice

To connect your sense of purpose to real actions, write out the following prompt ten times. Focus on small, practical ways you can help people at home, at work, or in your community:

"The people around me benefit when I use my ability to..."

Example responses to guide your writing:

- ...the people around me benefit when I use my ability to listen calmly to their concerns without trying to fix their problems immediately.
- ...the people around me benefit when I use my ability to organize chaotic tasks into clear, step-by-step lists at work.
- ...the people around me benefit when I use my ability to maintain a clean, orderly shared living space.
- ...the people around me benefit when I use my ability to offer steady, reliable assistance when heavy physical lifting or manual labor is needed.

After you've written your ten statements, pick one that you can act on right away. Write down one small, specific way you'll put it into practice this week.

To make sure your action is based on self-trust and not just trying to please others, use the "Purpose Test." Check that your action meets at least two of these:

- **Growth**: does it push you to learn or handle discomfort?
- **Service**: does it help someone else?

- **Connection**: does it involve honest communication or teamwork?
- **Responsibility**: are you taking ownership, even if it gets tough?

Troubleshooting

"But I Have Wasted Too Much Time"

It's normal to feel sad, regretful, or even angry when you think about years spent avoiding challenges or staying in your comfort zone. Don't try to cover up these feelings with empty sayings like "*everything happens for a reason*" or "*it's never too late to have a perfect life.*"

The time you lost avoiding challenges is gone, and it's okay to feel that loss. But letting regret keep you from moving forward is just another way to stay stuck. If you tell yourself there's no point in trying because you can't have a perfect record, you end up staying on the sidelines.

Focus on what you can do now, not on the past you can't change. Ask yourself honestly: "*Given my age, resources, and real limitations, what choices can I make this year to make it count*?" You can't get back lost years, but you can make sure they don't take away from the time you still have.

"My Work Is Not Meaningful"

Many people feel disconnected because their jobs seem repetitive or lack deeper meaning. If your work doesn't feel meaningful, don't quit on impulse to chase a perfect passion. That can lead to financial problems and make it even harder to trust yourself.

Remember, your job doesn't have to give your whole life meaning to be valuable. It can be a steady, respectable way to support yourself, set boundaries, and give you the resources to find meaning in other parts of your life.

Start by looking for ways to make your current job more meaningful. Set healthy boundaries, do your work with care, treat coworkers with respect, and avoid office gossip or grudges about extra hours.

Also, look beyond your main job. You can create, teach, or help others in your free time. Volunteer locally, learn a new skill at home, help a neighbor, or coach a youth team. Purpose isn't about your job title; it's about how you show up and take responsibility in everyday life.

Chapter 9 Checklist

Review your progress over the last three days and verify that you have completed each of the following behavioral milestones. Do not move forward until you can check off each item with concrete, written proof of performance:

☐ **Selected a 30-Hour Competence-Building Project**: I have chosen one specific, physical, or technical skill, defined a five-hour milestone, and established a realistic weekly practice schedule.
☐ **Completed One Career or Life Action Step**: I have taken one concrete, real-world professional or administrative action (such as updating my resume, applying for a role, or scheduling a health check-up) to create actual physical movement.
☐ **Wrote and Acted on a Contribution Statement**: I have identified how the people around me benefit from my skills, selected one small way to contribute this week, and verified that it meets the criteria of the Purpose Test.
☐ **Decoupled Achievement from Basic Human Worth**: I have written down and acknowledged that my moral value as a person remains constant, regardless of whether my skill practice is awkward or my career applications are rejected.
☐ **Chosen Active Participation over Endless

Preparation: I have closed my re tabs, stopped planning for perfect conditions, and initiated my first practice session or career action while still feeling like a beginner.

Chapter Ten

Build Connection and Become a Man You Can Rely On

Narrative Opening

Ethan notices he's been hoping a romantic relationship or a great group of friends would appear. But he hasn't reached out or supported other men at all. Sitting alone in his apartment, he sees that his isolation isn't just bad luck; it's something he's kept going by waiting for others to make the first move.

Marcus checks his contacts and sees that for fifteen years, his ex-wife made all their social plans. He hasn't called his old college roommate or close friends in over a year and a half, thinking they're too busy or would have called if they wanted to talk. By getting comfortable at home and then becoming isolated, he's let his friendships fade away.

Both men are feeling the results of being passive about friendship. They treated friendships like something that would happen on its own, instead of something you have to build. Recognizing this can inspire men to feel hopeful and motivated to take action to become someone others can count on.

Why Men Need Real Connection

Most men don't choose to be isolated; it just happens slowly over time. Work, relationships, and family often take over, and friendships get pushed aside. But facing life's challenges without close friends makes things harder. Without reliable male friendships, you miss out on advice, honest feedback, and people to share the load with.

Five specific challenges characterize how men struggle with connection:

1. **Relying Only on Shared Activities**: Many men's friendships are built around things like watching sports, playing games, or working on projects. These are good ways to connect, but they can also act as a shield. If the activity ends, so does the friendship. Often, men know what their friends think about a team or a tool, but not what they're struggling with or working on in life.

2. **Hiding Struggles Behind Success**: Many men only show their achievements to others, like promotions, new purchases, or fitness wins. But they keep worries about money, relationships, or not being good enough to themselves. This makes everyone feel alone in their struggles, thinking they're the only one having a hard time.

3. **Fear of Looking Weak or Needy**: Worrying about seeming weak or like a burden stops many men from reaching out when they're stressed. To overcome this, practice sharing small, honest thoughts or feelings gradually, which builds trust and reduces fear. Remember, vulnerability is a strength that fosters genuine connections.

4. **Relying Only on Romantic Partners for Support**: Without close friends, men often turn to their partner for all their emotional needs. This puts too much pressure on one

relationship. Your partner ends up being your therapist, advisor, teammate, and main source of support, which can throw things out of balance.

5. **Letting Friendships Fade After Big Life Changes**: Moving, getting married, changing jobs, or going through a divorce can all make friendships drift apart unless you make an effort. It's easy to think a friend doesn't care if they haven't called, but they're probably feeling the same hesitation you are.

To really trust yourself, stop seeing isolation as protection. It's actually a way of avoiding things that leaves you open to more self-doubt.

Friendship Requires Repetition

Making friends as an adult isn't as easy or automatic as it was in school or college. You can't count on living nearby or sharing a dorm to make connections happen. Instead, you need to learn and use the practical steps that help build adult friendships.

- **Proximity**: You must physically put yourself in environments where the same people gather regularly. This could be a local gym, a professional association, a hobby group, a volunteer organization, or a neighborhood association. Merely attending once is not enough; you must establish a recognizable presence.

- **Repeated Contact**: Trust grows when you see people regularly. Studies show it takes many hours of casual time together to turn an acquaintance into a friend. Keep showing up so people get used to having you around.

- **Shared Activities**: Working toward a common objective, whether it is training for an event, building a community project, learning a skill, or organizing an initiative, creates a low-friction environment where conversation can flow naturally without the pressure of forced face-to-face emotional dialogue. This can make men feel more connected and confident in their ability to form bonds.

- **Incremental Vulnerability**: Trust doesn't come from sharing your biggest problems right away. Start by sharing small, honest things, like an opinion or a personal goal, and see how the other person responds. If they're open and respectful, you can share a bit more next time.

- **Reliability**: If you say you'll be there, be there. If you offer to help, follow through. Being reliable means your actions match your words. When people see they can count on you, they'll trust you more.

- **The Courage to Initiate**: This is where most people get stuck. Many men wait for someone else to reach out first. When you take the first step, like sending a text or planning a meetup, you break the cycle. You might not always get a response, but that's a small risk for the chance at a real connection.

Day 28: Initiate One Connection

Confidence Rep

Today's task is to reach out to one friend, acquaintance, or coworker. Don't wait for them to contact you, and don't overthink what to say. Just suggest a simple, specific plan and send the message before you second-guess yourself.

Scripts to Use

- **Option A** (For an old friend or contact you have lost touch with): *"I've been meaning to catch up. Are you free for coffee next week?"*

- **Option B** (For an acquaintance, gym partner, or hobby

colleague): *"I'm trying to be more intentional about staying connected. Want to work out Saturday?"*

- **Option C** (For someone you recently met or want to get to know better): *"I enjoyed talking with you. I'm going to that event again next week if you'd like to join."*

Rules for the Rep

1. **Send your message before you edit it more than twice**. Over-editing is just another way of worrying about getting a perfect reply. Keep it simple, direct, and short.

2. **Be specific with your invitation**. Instead of saying, *"We should hang out sometime,"* suggest an actual activity and a general time, like *"coffee next week"* or *"workout Saturday."* This makes it easier for the other person to agree or offer another idea.

3. **Accept their answer without taking it personally**. If they're too busy, say, *"No worries, let's try another time."* If they don't reply, take it as a sign they're busy right now, not as a judgment about you.

Day 29: Share One Level Deeper

Confidence Rep

Today, try sharing something a bit more honest and personal than usual with someone you trust, a friend, family member, or reliable coworker. Take one step down the vulnerability ladder.

The Gradual Vulnerability Ladder

Review these six levels of communication, moving from lowest risk to deepest connection:

1. **Clichés and Small Talk**: Standard, polite greetings and superficial exchanges.
2. **Facts and Information**: Sharing objective data, news, or logistics without personal commentary.
3. **Opinions and Ideas**: Expressing your thoughts, beliefs, or intellectual perspectives on a topic.
4. **Hopes and Dreams**: Revealing your personal goals, aspirations, and what drives you.
5. **Feelings and Emotions**: Sharing your current emotional state, vulnerabilities, and how you are actually feeling.
6. **Complete Authenticity and Raw Vulnerability**: Disclosing your deepest fears, struggles, and core truths with absolute honesty.

Action Step

Think about what you usually talk about with this person. If it's mostly sports or work (Level 1), today your goal is to share something at Level 2 or 3.

For example, you might say: "*I'm actually working on improving my physical consistency this month, and it's been tougher than I expected to get to the gym after work.*"

Pay attention to how it feels to let someone see you a little more honestly. Notice that nothing bad happens when you admit you don't have it all together.

Day 30: Write Your Personal Code

Five-Minute Practice

You build self-trust by having a clear, written set of standards you stick to, no matter what's going on around you or how you feel. Today, write down five to ten personal standards. These aren't just wishes; they're statements about the kind of man you're becoming through your daily actions.

Use the specific starter formula: "*I am becoming a man who...*" to define your non-negotiables. Write these down in a journal, keep them somewhere you'll see them, and read them every morning to set the tone for your day.

> "*I am becoming a man who speaks honestly and directly before resentment has a chance to build.*"
>
> "*I am becoming a man who treats rejection and criticism as painful information, not an identity verdict.*"
>
> "*I am becoming a man who allows himself to be a beginner so that he can build real competence.*"
>
> "*I am becoming a man who refuses to abandon himself or run away when discomfort appears.*"
>
> "*I am becoming a man who takes responsibility for initiating connection instead of waiting in isolation.*"

"I am becoming a man who sets clear boundaries and tolerates the temporary guilt of saying no."

Write your personal standards in a notebook, on an index card, or in a digital file you can easily find. These will guide you when you hit tough times or start to doubt yourself.

The Final Proof Review

Now that you've finished this 30-day plan, it's time to look back and see how far you've come. Don't judge your progress by how confident or happy you feel. Instead, look at the real actions and changes you've made over the past month.

Baseline Comparison

Review your actions from Day 1 to Day 30 and complete the following progress assessment:

Behavioral Marker

Promises Kept
Day 1: How many small promises did you keep to yourself per week?

____

Day 30: How many small promises did you keep to yourself per week?

____

Independent Choices
Day 1: Did you poll others or seek permission for minor decisions?

____

Day 30: Did you make choices and allow them to be yours without polling? __________

Discomfort Rungs Climbed
Day 1: Did you run from uncomfortable social or professional situations?

____

Day 30: Did you enter uncomfortable situations and stay 5 minutes longer? __________

Preferences & Boundaries

Day 1: Did you agree with others to avoid conflict or keep the peace? __________

Day 30: Did you state a preference or say "no" using a clean script? __________

Rejections Handled

Day 1: Did a rejection or failure spiral into a weeks-long identity verdict? __________

Day 30: Did you use the 24-Hour Recovery Protocol to maintain momentum? __________

Connections Initiated

Day 1: Did you wait in isolation for others to reach out to you? __________

Day 30: Did you actively initiate a connection or share a level deeper? __________

Workbook Prompts

Take a moment to think honestly about your last 30 days and answer these four key questions:

1. **Which specific action over the last 30 days made you feel the strongest sense of quiet pride?**
   – Write down the exact date, event, and choice you made. What did this choice prove to you about your capabilities?

2. **What is the most challenging situation you survived or stayed in during this plan that you would have previously avoided?**
   – How did your mind try to convince you to escape, and how did

you handle the physical discomfort without leaving?

3. **In what areas do you still notice a tendency to self-abandon, appease others, or seek external validation?**
   – Identify the specific triggers (e.g., certain people, professional pressures, dating settings) where you must remain highly vigilant.
4. **What is the next piece of behavioral proof you want to build over the coming months?**
   – Define one concrete, manageable habit or confidence rep that will support your ongoing path of self-trust.

Troubleshooting

"What if I tried to initiate connection and got ignored or rejected?"

This is a normal part of making connections. If someone doesn't reply or politely says no, it's not a judgment on your worth or your ability as a friend. It just means they're busy or have other things going on right now.

When this happens, don't pull back or tell yourself, "*See? I shouldn't have tried.*" Instead, remind yourself: I took the step. I showed interest. I survived the silence. I'm still here, and I'm still supporting myself.

Your job is to keep reaching out, not to control how others respond.

"What if I feel like my personal code is too demanding and I keep failing to meet it?"

If you keep falling short of your standards, you might have set them as impossible goals instead of helpful directions. For example, "*I am becoming a man who never makes mistakes*" just sets you up for self-criticism.

Review your code and make sure each standard is about how you respond to challenges, not about being perfect. For example, instead of "*I am becoming a man who never gets anxious,*" try "*I am becoming a man who takes action even when I feel anxious.*"

If you slip up, don't call yourself a failure. Use the Clean Restart: say what happened, figure out what got in the way, adjust your plan, and take the next step.

"How do I avoid slipping back into my old habits of isolation and people-pleasing now that the 30 days are over?"

You fall back into old habits when you stop tracking your progress and hope motivation will last. To avoid this, treat self-trust like a relationship that needs regular care.

Keep using what you've learned: set one small, believable promise each week and track it. Keep your Personal Code where you can see it every day. Do a weekly review and write down three real actions you took. Use your boundary scripts, and see any guilt as a sign you're growing, not a reason to back off.

Chapter 10 Checklist

Review your performance for this final chapter of the action plan. Check off each item as you complete it to secure your final pieces of behavioral proof:

1. Read your Personal Code aloud every morning to reinforce your commitment.
2. Log your three pieces of behavioral proof in your success journal during your weekly review.
3. Use your boundary scripts in a real-world scenario, successfully leaning into the discomfort of guilt.

4. Celebrate your progress and acknowledge the shift in your self-identity.

***

☐ **Initiated one meaningful connection**: You sent a direct, specific invitation to a friend, colleague, or acquaintance without over-editing the message.
☐ **Shared something more honestly than usual**: You moved one step down the gradual vulnerability ladder with a safe person, letting yourself be seen more clearly.
☐ **Completed my Personal Code**: You drafted five to ten personal standards starting with "I am becoming a man who..." and recorded them in a secure place.
☐ **Completed the final baseline comparison**: You quantitatively evaluated your progress across the six behavioral markers from Day 1 to Day 30.
☐ **Selected habits/relationships to support my ongoing path**: You identified your next steps, recognized your remaining triggers for self-abandonment, and committed to a specific plan to maintain your momentum.

Conclusion

You do not need to feel fearless; you need to know that showing up is a true sign of your strength and progress.

Closing Narrative

Ethan waits outside the local community center, where a social event is happening. His hands are a bit sweaty, and his chest feels tight, just like before. In the past, he would have sat in his car for forty minutes, hoping his anxiety would fade, then left without going in. This time, he doesn't wait for perfect confidence. He turns off the car, gets out, and walks straight inside.

Once inside, Ethan starts a conversation near the refreshment table. At first, things feel awkward; he misunderstands a comment and feels self-conscious. But he doesn't leave. Soon, he finds himself chatting easily with someone else, and they laugh together about something they both enjoy. Before they part, Ethan asks if she'd like to meet for coffee later in the week. She smiles and says she has a busy work schedule, leaving her answer open.

Ethan feels disappointed right away. As he heads to his car at the end of the night, he doesn't judge himself or think he's foolish for trying. Instead, he writes down what he did: he went to the event, took part, showed honest interest, handled a vague answer without falling apart, and supported himself through it all.

On Friday afternoon, Marcus gets a text from a relative asking him to spend Saturday helping with a household chore that isn't urgent. In the past, he would have quickly said, "Sure, no problem," and then spent the weekend feeling resentful. This time, Marcus stops to check his own plans, which include visiting his brother.

He writes back using the boundaries he's learned: *"I can't do that this weekend, but I can discuss helping you next month if you still need it."* After he sends the message, his relative replies with a short, disappointed note. Marcus feels a wave of guilt, but he reminds himself this feeling is normal and doesn't mean he's done something wrong. He sits with the discomfort and sticks to his decision.

The next day, Marcus has lunch with an old college friend. For the first time in a year and a half, he doesn't pretend everything is perfect. He talks honestly about his divorce, recent job changes, and what he's doing to move forward. He doesn't look for pity or ask to be rescued; he shares his story. Marcus still feels some insecurity and sadness, but he is no longer hiding from his own life.

What Has Actually Changed

After finishing a structured program like this 30-day action plan, it's normal to hope for a big change. You might think you'll wake up on Day 31 feeling fearless, without any doubts, and safe from rejection.

While feelings of vulnerability and fear of rejection may still arise, remember that these are normal. The goal isn't to eliminate these feelings but to learn how to handle them with resilience and self-compassion, so they don't hinder your progress.

Understanding that feelings of vulnerability and anxiety may persist is normal. Focus on how you respond-by practicing self-compassion and using coping strategies-so these emotions don't control your actions or self-esteem.

Now, these feelings don't control what you do. Over the past thirty days, you've shown yourself that you can feel anxious and still act, which boosts your confidence and sense of control.

Signs of Progress That Do Not Feel Dramatic

Real progress shows up in small, practical changes in your daily life, making you feel hopeful and motivated by tangible steps.

Some signs of lasting progress are: You react less emotionally and choose how to respond. You can handle discomfort without giving up on your plans. You focus on steady, daily actions instead of pushing yourself too hard all at once. Your self-talk is more helpful and focused on solving problems, not criticizing yourself.

- **Reduced Recovery Time**: When a setback or rejection occurs, you no longer spiral into a week-long period of isolation or self-attack. You stabilize, apply a recovery protocol, and return to your routine within twenty-four hours.
- **Unrehearsed Preference Stating**: You state what you want, what you think, or where you want to eat without spending ten minutes mentally rehearsing the words or adding qualifying apologies to your sentences.
- **Conscious Comparison Interruption**: You catch yourself scrolling through social media or comparing your life to a colleague's, recognize the comparison trigger, and intentionally close the application or redirect your focus to your own tasks.
- **Immediate Restarts**: After missing a habit, a workout, or a

daily promise, you do not wait until next Monday or declare the entire system broken. You complete the very next available representative action.

- **Unconditional Compliment Acceptance**: When someone offers you genuine appreciation or feedback, you say, "Thank you," instead of explaining why you do not deserve the praise or pointing out your flaws.
- **Active Assistance Seeking**: You ask for support, advice, or feedback from a position of self-respect, rather than viewing the request as an admission of weakness or failure.
- **Early Departure from Detrimental Environments**: You quietly exit conversations, relationships, or situations where your boundaries are consistently dismissed, rather than staying to argue or attempt to win approval.
- **Tolerating Disappointment in Others**: You can say no to a request and allow another person to feel disappointed without rushing in to rescue them, apologize excessively, or change your mind.

The Next 90 Days

To move from a 30-day program to lasting change, you need a plan you can keep up with. The next ninety days are split into three months, each with a focus: keeping your habits steady, growing your abilities, and bringing your values into your community.

Month One: Stabilize

The main goal for the first month is to keep your progress going without burning out. Each day, keep one small promise to yourself that takes less than ten minutes, like stretching, journaling, or leaving your phone out of your bedroom. Each week, do one thing that makes you a bit uncomfortable from your list. Have at least one honest conversation a week where you share what you want, set a boundary, or tell the truth about something personal. Every Sunday, spend fifteen minutes looking back at what you did, the promises you kept, and how you handled any setbacks.

Month Two: Expand

In the second month, start making your commitments a bit bigger and harder. Move up two steps on your discomfort ladder and try situations that need more openness or social courage. Pick one area of your life where your boundaries are weak and set a clear rule for yourself. Spend at least three hours a week working on the skill-building project you chose earlier, and keep track of your practice time. Be more honest in your close relationships by sharing your goals, values, or struggles without trying to impress anyone.

Month Three: Lead

In the last month, focus on helping others and building trust through service and responsibility. Look for ways to support a coworker or family member, like mentoring, helping with a project, or just listening without giving advice. Take on a small project or activity in your community, workplace, or hobby group. Practice letting others speak honestly without judging or competing. Finally, review your personal standards and update your code of conduct to match where you are now.

When Professional Support Is Appropriate

Building self-trust by taking action is a powerful way to grow, but it doesn't replace professional mental health care. Real self-trust means knowing your limits and reaching out for expert help when you need it.

If you experience any of the following challenges, seeking the guidance of a licensed therapist, counselor, or medical professional is the most responsible action you can take:

- **Persistent Clinical Depression**: Feelings of emptiness, hopelessness, or severe lethargy that persist for more than two consecutive weeks and interfere with your basic ability to work, eat, or sleep.

- **Unresolved Trauma**: Flashbacks, intrusive thoughts, extreme hypervigilance, or panic attacks related to past physical, emotional, or psychological trauma.

- **Substance Dependence**: Using alcohol, drugs, or compulsive behaviors to numb anxiety, manage stress, or escape uncomfortable realities.

- **Severe Emotional Dysregulation**: Explosive, unpredictable anger or rage that damages your relationships, employment, or physical safety.

- **Prolonged, Paralyzing Grief**: A sense of loss from a divorce, bereavement, or life transition that prevents you from engaging in basic daily activities months after the event.

- **Self-Harm or Suicidal Ideation**: Any thoughts of ending your life or harming yourself. (If you are in crisis, please utilize immediate emergency services or national crisis hotlines).

Deciding to go to therapy is not a failure or a weakness. It's a strong, thoughtful choice to get professional help for deep issues, so you can get back to building your life with more clarity and strength.

Final Letter to the Reader

You never had to be the loudest, richest, strongest, or most powerful person in the room to have dignity. You don't need to act, pretend, or put on a tough front to earn your own respect.

You were asked to stop disappearing from your own life.

Self-esteem isn't something magical that appears when you reach a perfect goal. It's a real, ongoing relationship with yourself, built through many small, everyday choices. Each time you tell the truth instead of just pleasing others, keep a promise to yourself, face discomfort to stand up for yourself, or start again after a setback, you prove to yourself that you can be trusted.

The point of this work isn't to promise you'll never feel disappointment, rejection, or pain. The real goal is to know, deep down, that no matter what happens, you'll show up, handle it, and stay true to yourself. Your proof is real. Your actions belong to you. Keep building your evidence, one step at a time.

A Personal Request from the Author

Building self-esteem is not about becoming fearless, perfect, or unaffected by life. It is about learning to trust yourself, respect your needs, recover from setbacks, and keep showing up, even when you feel uncertain.

Throughout these 30 days, you have practiced making self-directed choices, keeping small promises, setting boundaries, handling rejection, building healthier relationships, strengthening your competence, and creating a personal code you can rely on.

More men may benefit from these lessons, tools, scripts, worksheets, and daily exercises, but they may need your help finding them.

If you found this book worthwhile, practical, or informative, please consider leaving an honest review. Your experience may help another man recognize that he is not alone, that change is possible, and that genuine strength begins with taking one honest step forward.

Thank you for reading and for helping this message reach others who may need it.

- George Munson

Supplemental Resources

Boundary Script Library

This library provides direct, non-manipulative language to protect your time and energy. These scripts are not designed to dominate or lecture others; they are clean, objective statements of your capacity and limits.

Declining Over-Commitments

Use these when you cannot take on another task without sacrificing your existing priorities or well-being.

The Direct No: "I *can't take that on right now. My schedule is fully committed.*"
The Warm Alternative: "*Thank you for thinking of me, but I don't have the capacity to do this justice. I have to pass.*"
The Conditional Offer: "*I can't help with the whole project, but I can dedicate one hour on Thursday to review your draft.*"

Delaying Answers

Use these to interrupt the impulse to say "yes" immediately out of anxiety or pressure.

The Calendar Check: *"I need to check my schedule and commitments first. I'll get back to you by tomorrow morning."*
The Decision Pause: *"I want to give this some thought before deciding. Let me review my capacity and let you know on Friday."*
The Boundary Pause: *"I'm not in a position to agree to this right now. Let me sleep on it and get back to you."*

Correcting Disrespect

Use these to address inappropriate behavior or language calmly, without escalating into conflict or shrinking into appeasement.

The Interruption: *"Please don't raise your voice to me. I want to resolve this, but we need to speak calmly."*
The Direct Feedback: *"I'm happy to discuss constructive feedback, but personal insults don't work for me."*
The Boundary Restatement: *"We disagree, but I expect us to speak to each other with mutual respect."*

Handling Workplace Overload

Use these to negotiate workload realistically with managers or colleagues without sounding incompetent.

The Prioritization Request: *"I have the bandwidth to complete either Project A or Project B by Friday, but not both. Which one should I prioritize?"*
The Capacity Alert: *"Adding this task means the delivery date for the current project will slip by three days. How would you like me to proceed?"*
The Clear Limit: *"I can complete this analysis, but I will need to hand off my administrative tasks to someone else this week to make it happen."*

Relationship Communication Scripts

These direct, non-manipulative templates will help you communicate clearly under pressure. They are designed to express your perspective honestly, without passive people-pleasing, aggressive posturing, or game-playing.

Expressing Romantic Interest

Use clear, direct language that communicates your interest without putting the other person on a pedestal or hiding behind casual indifference.

Direct Invitation: *"I've really enjoyed talking with you. I'd like to take you out for a drink or coffee this week. How does Thursday evening look for you?"*
The Follow-Up: *"I had a great time tonight. I'd definitely like to see you again. Let's plan something for next weekend."*

Accepting Rejection Gracefully

Preserve your dignity and respect her boundary by closing the interaction cleanly, without seeking a justification or showing resentment.

Initial Response: *"I appreciate you being direct with me. Thank you for letting me know, and I wish you the best."*
When Moving on from a Casual Connection: *"Thanks for the clarity. I've enjoyed getting to know you, but I respect your decision."*

Requesting Reassurance Responsibly

State your feelings honestly without making your partner responsible for fixing your internal anxiety or demanding that they prove their commitment.

The Vulnerable Ownership Script: *"I've noticed some old insecurities coming up for me today, and I'm feeling a bit disconnected. I know this is* *mine to work through, but I'd appreciate a little reassurance or just some quiet time together tonight."*

Seeking Clarity: *"I'm feeling a bit anxious about where we stand. Can we talk for a few minutes so I can check in and make sure we're good?"*

Discussing Jealousy

Address jealous feelings constructively by naming the emotion and discussing the objective behavior, rather than accusing, tracking, or controlling your partner.

The Non-Accusatory Opener: *"I noticed some jealousy coming up for me when you were talking with your ex earlier. I don't want to micromanage your friendships, but I'd like to talk about what happened so I can process it and understand our boundaries better."*

Rejection Recovery Card

When a setback, rejection, or failure threatens to trigger a downward spiral, execute the four steps of the 24-Hour Recovery Protocol immediately.

THE 24-HOUR RECOVERY PROTOCOL

1. STABILIZE (Hours 0–4)

• **Action**: Halt all impulsive texts, emails, or calls. Do not make any global conclusions about your worth, intelligence, or future.
• **Check**: Have you eaten, hydrated, and slept? Move your body for 10 minutes before responding.

2. DESCRIBE (Hours 4–12)

• **Action**: Strip away the dramatic narrative. Write down the raw, objective facts of what happened in 5 sentences or fewer.
• **Check**: What are the known facts? (e.g., "*The client chose another vendor.* ") What is a manufactured verdict? (e.g., "*I am bad at my jo*b." - Cross this out).

3. LEARN (Hours 12–18)

• **Action**: Extract one practical, actionable lesson from the event.
• **Check**: What can I improve next time? If the outcome was due to simple incompatibility or timing, accept it as neutral data.

4. RE-ENTER (Hours 18–24)

• **Action**: Make one small, constructive choice completely unrelated to the setback.
• **Check**: Complete a micro-rep (e.g., clear your desk, go to the gym, or reply to a pending email) to prove that the setback does not run your life.

Personal Standards Worksheet

Your personal standards are not a wishlist of external results; they are the baseline behaviors you commit to maintaining, regardless of how you feel or what others do. Use this worksheet to define your core standards. Instead of writing passive goals ("I want to be fit"), write active, identity-shifting declarations using the formula: "I am becoming a man who..."

1. Health & Physical Care

Focus on stewardship, sleep, movement, and physical self-respect.
Standard: I am becoming a man who __________
The Minimum Weekly Action: __________

2. Career & Professional Integrity

Focus on daily effort, skill development, and clean communication.
Standard: I am becoming a man who __________
The Minimum Weekly Action: __________

3. Finances & Resource Stewardship

Focus on tracking, intentional spending, and proactive planning.
Standard: I am becoming a man who __________
The Minimum Weekly Action: __________

4. Friendship & Connection

Focus on initiation, reliability, and gradual, honest vulnerability.
Standard: I am becoming a man who __________
The Minimum Weekly Action: __________

5. Family & Intimate Relationships

Focus on setting clear boundaries, eliminating appeasement, and showing up honestly.
Standard: I am becoming a man who __________
The Minimum Weekly Action: __________

The Commitment: When you fail to meet a standard, do not run a trial on your character. Use the clean restart: acknowledge the slip, adjust the friction in your environment, and execute the next available minimum action. Your proof is built in the recovery.

Support Map

This worksheet maps your interpersonal environment to ensure you have the resources to grow while protecting your energy. On a blank sheet of paper, sketch five concentric circles and place your connections into the following categories:

1. The Core (Personal Network)

Identify 1–3 people who have earned the right to hear your unfinished thoughts. These are individuals who offer objective feedback without rescuing or judging you.
Names: __________
Next Rep: Reach out this week to schedule a low-stakes catch-up.

2. Professional & Skill Mentors

List individuals who possess the specific competence you want to build. This is not for emotional processing, but for structured guidance.
Names/Roles: __________
Next Rep: Ask one specific, actionable question about their area of expertise.

3. Activity-Based Communities

Identify groups where connection is built through shared action rather than performance (e.g., local run clubs, volunteering, martial arts, or hobby classes).
Communities: __________
Next Rep: Attend one scheduled event and focus solely on participating as a beginner.

4. Boundary Adjustments

Identify relationships where your old pattern of people-pleasing or appeasement has bred resentment. These connections require clearer limits, not necessarily termination.

Names: __________

The Limit Needed: (e.g., *"I will decline last-minute weekend work requests."*) __________

The Support Rule: You do not need a massive social circle. You need a functional network where your boundaries are clear, your competence is challenged, and your self-trust is supported by honest evidence.

Men's Group Discussion Guide

This guide is designed to facilitate honest, ego-free conversations. Whether you are meeting in a veterans' hall, a church basement, a professional development circle, or a casual backyard, use these questions to cut through surface-level posturing and focus on behavioral proof.

Introduction: You Do Not Need More Hype, You Need Evidence

1. How has the "hype-and-crash" cycle of motivational content affected your self-trust in the past?
2. Looking at Ethan and Marcus, which pattern of self-abandonment do you fall into most often: avoidance (disappearing) or appeasement (people-pleasing)?

Chapter 1: Stop Outsourcing Your Worth

1. What is the primary external metric (e.g., bank account, career title, dating success, or social status) that you have allowed to be an "identity verdict" for your life?
2. Share one conditional rule you have placed on your self-respect (e.g., "I will finally respect myself when..."). How has that moving finish line affected you?

Chapter 2: Stop Rejecting Yourself First

1. What does your "inner prosecutor" sound like when you make a mistake? What is its favorite recurring accusation?
2. Why does rejecting yourself first feel safer than letting the world reject you? How can we help each other catch this pattern this week?

Chapter 3: Keep Small Promises and Build Self-Trust

1. We often set massive, unsustainable goals as an emotional escape hatch to feel better temporarily. What is one over-ambitious plan you recently abandoned?
2. What is the "minimum believable promise" you are committing to for the next seven days? How will you handle a miss without slipping into self-attack?

Chapter 4: Enter Life Before You Feel Ready

1. Where in your life are you currently waiting to "feel ready" or "feel confident" before taking action?
2. Describe a recent "awkward" social interaction. How can we reframe that moment as a successful behavioral repetition rather than a failure?

Chapter 5: Respect Your Body Without Making It Your Verdict

1. What modern comparison engines (social media accounts, peer groups, or cultural standards) trigger your physical insecurities the most?
2. What does physical stewardship look like for you when it is based on self-respect rather than self-punishment?

Chapter 6: Say What You Mean and Set Boundaries

1. In what relationships do you find yourself signing the "people-pleasing contract" (suppressing your needs to avoid conflict)? What resentment has this built?
2. Practice saying "no" to a hypothetical request using one of the clean scripts from this chapter. How does tolerating the immediate guilt feel?

Chapter 7: Handle Rejection, Criticism, and Failure Without Collapsing

1. Think of a recent rejection or professional setback. What was the raw fact, and what was the "catastrophic story" your mind attached to it?
2. Who is one person in this group you can commit to contacting during your next 24-Hour Recovery Protocol?

Chapter 8: Build Relationships Without Neediness or Performance

1. What does "performing for selection" look like in your romantic, social, or professional life? How does it prevent genuine connection?
2. How do you distinguish between having normal human needs and practicing "neediness" in your current relationships?

Chapter 9: Build Competence and Purpose Without Worshipping Achievement

1. What is a 30-hour skill you want to develop, and what specific "beginner embarrassment" must you tolerate to start?
2. If your current career or role does not feel deeply meaningful, how can you build a sense of purpose through small acts of service or contribution outside of work?

Chapter 10 & Conclusion: Build Connection and Become a Man You Can Rely On

1. Why is it historically difficult for men to maintain friendships as they age? What is one practical step we can take to keep this group active and reliable?
2. Read your "Personal Code" ("I am becoming a man who...") aloud to the group. How will you hold yourself accountable to these standards this month?

End-of-Book Self-Trust Assessment

This assessment is identical to the one you completed on Day 1. By answering these questions honestly based on your behavior over the past week, rather than your aspirations or history, you will generate a clear, quantitative map of your progress and identify your next developmental focus.

The Self-Trust Inventory

For each statement, score yourself from **1** to **5**:

1: Never / Strongly Disagree
2: Rarely / Disagree
3: Sometimes / Neutral
4: Usually / Agree
5: Consistently / Strongly Agree

Category A: Behavioral Proof & Promises

1. I keep the small promises I make to myself, even when my motivation drops. [ ]
2. I make decisions without polling others or seeking immediate reassurance. [ ]
3. When I miss a habit, I execute a clean restart without criticizing my character. [ ]

Category A Subtotal: __________ / 15

Category B: Exposure & Discomfort

4. I enter uncomfortable social or professional situations before I feel fully ready. [ ]

5. I allow myself to be seen as a beginner when learning a new skill. [ ]
6. I stay in awkward or tense moments rather than escaping or using my phone. [ ]

Category B Subtotal: _____________ ___ / 15

Category C: Boundaries & Assertiveness

7. I decline requests that cross my boundaries without over-explaining or apologizing. [ ]
8. I state my preferences clearly, even when they conflict with the group's opinion. [ ]
9. I express my needs and vulnerabilities without demanding emotional rescue. [ ]

Category C Subtotal: ___________ / 15

Category D: Setback Resilience

10. I recover from rejection or criticism without entering an identity-verdict spiral. [ ]
11. I actively seek and listen to constructive feedback from trusted peers. [ ]
12. I treat bad results as objective information rather than a moral score. [ ]

Category D Subtotal: ___________ / 15

Score Comparison & Action Plan

Transfer your Day 1 and Day 30 scores to the table below to measure your growth.

A: Promises & Decisions

Day 1 Score __________/ 15
Day 30 Score __________/ 15
Net Change (+/-) __________

B: Discomfort & Exposure

Day 1 Score __________/ 15
Day 30 Score __________/ 15
Net Change (+/-) __________

C: Boundaries & Assertiveness

Day 1 Score __________/ 15
Day 30 Score __________/ 15
Net Change (+/-) __________

D: Setback Resilience

Day 1 Score __________/ 15
Day 30 Score __________/ 15
Net Change (+/-) __________

TOTAL SCORE

Day 1 Score __________/ 60
Day 30 Score __________/ 60
Net Change (+/-) __________

Interpreting Your Results:

• **Highest Score Category**: This is your current anchor. Use these strengths to support more challenging areas.

• **Lowest Score Category**: This is your primary developmental focus for the next 90 days.
- If Category C is lowest, prioritize the Boundary Script Library.
- If Category D is lowest, commit to the Rejection Recovery Protocol.

Words to Use

This appendix is your quick-access reference guide for the communication scripts detailed throughout this book. These words are designed to be plain, direct, and non-manipulative. They prioritize clear boundary-setting and vulnerability without falling into passive people-pleasing or aggressive posturing.

Chapter 2: Managing Self-Criticism & Public Situations

• **Accepting a Compliment**: *"Thank you. I appreciate you saying that."*
• **Responding to a Mistake**: *"I missed that. I'll correct it."*
• **Acknowledging Nervousness**: *"I'm a little nervous, but I still wanted to be here."*
• **Replacing Self-Deprecation**: *"I'm still learning how this works."* (Instead of: *"I'm an idiot with this stuff."*)

Chapter 4: Social Interactions & Joining Groups

• **Entering a Conversation**: *"How do you know the host?"*
• **Joining a Group**: *"Mind if I join you?"*
• **Asking a Question**: *"I may be missing something. Could you explain that part?"*
• **Admitting Inexperience**: *"I'm new to this, so I'm still learning."*

Chapter 6: Setting Boundaries & Declining Requests

• **Stating a Simple Preference**:
– *"I would rather eat somewhere quieter."*
– *"I prefer Saturday."*
– *"I don't agree with that."*
– *"I'd like some time to think."*
– *"That option doesn't work for me."*
• **Declining an Optional Commitment: Basic**:

– **Basic**: *"I can't take that on."*
– **Warm**: *"I appreciate you asking, but I'm not available."*
– **Alternative**: *"I can't do Friday, but I could help for an hour on Sunday."*
• **Expressing a Personal Need**:
– *" When plans change without notice, I feel disregarded. Please tell me as soon as you know."*
– *"I have been overwhelmed, and I need an evening without additional commitments."*

Chapter 8: Dating, Romance, & Vulnerability

• **Expressing Honest Interest**: *"I've enjoyed talking with you. Would you like to get coffee this week?"*
• **Naming an Insecurity Without Demanding Rescue**: *"I noticed I've been feeling insecure about this. I'm working on how I respond, but I wanted to be honest rather than act distant."*
• **Asking for Reassurance Responsibly**: *"I could use some reassurance, but I also know this feeling is mine to work through."*
• **Discussing Jealousy**: *"I noticed jealousy coming up. I don't want to accuse you, so I'd like to talk about what happened and what each of us needs."*
• **Accepting Romantic Rejection**: *"Thank you for being clear. I respect your decision."*

Chapter 10: Building Connection & Adult Friendships

• **Initiating a Casual Catch-Up**: *"I've been meaning to catch up. Are you free for coffee next week?"*
• **Proposing a Shared Activity**: *"I'm trying to be more intentional about staying connected. Want to work out Saturday?"*
• **Inviting Someone to an Event**: *"I enjoyed talking with you. I'm going to that event again next week if you'd like to join."*

What to Do After a Bad Week

A bad week is not a verdict on your character; it is a standard data point in any active life. When illness, travel, crisis, or a temporary relapse derails your momentum, the goal is not to execute a flawless recovery. The goal is to prevent a three-day slip from turning into a three-month abandonment of yourself.

Use this four-step protocol to reset without self-punishment.

1. Declare a Zero-Penalty Truce

The moment you realize you have slipped, the inner prosecutor will attempt to use your absence as evidence of permanent failure. Shut down this trial immediately. Do not try to "make up" for missed days by doubling your workouts, reading twice as many pages, or setting extreme goals for the coming week. This overcorrection is an emotional escape hatch that inevitably leads to another crash. Do not wait for next Monday, the first of the month, or a "perfect" day to restart. Say this to yourself:

> *"I went off track. It is a normal occurrence, not a character defect. My transition back starts with the next decision."*

2. Lower the Bar to a "Minimum Believable Rep"

When returning from a disruption, your cognitive and physical energy levels are depleted. Do not expect yourself to jump back into the program at full capacity. Strip the daily missions down to their absolute baseline. If you missed a week of the 30-day plan, do not try to complete three days of content in one afternoon. Pick one micro-action that takes less than five minutes and requires almost zero willpower. Examples:

Lay out your clothes for tomorrow
Drink one glass of water
Write down a single fact-feeling-verdict breakdown
Send one short, overdue email.

3. Conduct a No-Blame Audit

Once you have completed your single micro-rep, objectively evaluate what disrupted so you can design around it next time. Ask yourself:

"*What was the actual bottleneck*?" (e.g., "I caught a virus," "*My flight was delayed,*" "*I felt overwhelmed by the social exposure ladder and shut down.*")

"*How can I adjust the friction*?" (e.g., "*If I travel next week, I will plan for a 5-minute stretching routine in my hotel room instead of trying to find a gym.*")

4. Record the Restart

Your self-esteem is built on proof, and restarting after a failure is the highest-leverage proof you can collect. Enter your restart in your ledger. By resuming the program when you feel tired, awkward, or behind, you prove that your commitment is stronger than your need for a perfect record.

Available Professional Resources

If the tools in this plan bring up deep-seated trauma, persistent depression, or patterns of behavior that feel too heavy to carry alone, seeking professional care is not a sign of failure, but an act of high-integrity leadership.

The following verified, evidence-informed resources can help you find licensed mental health professionals, peer support networks, and immediate crisis assistance:

Finding a Licensed Therapist

• **Psychology Today Directory (psychologytoday.com)**: A comprehensive, searchable database of licensed psychologists, clinical social workers, and counselors. You can filter search results by location, insurance, and areas of expertise (such as men's issues, trauma, or anxiety).

• **National Alliance on Mental Illness (NAMI) (nami.org)**: Offers extensive educational resources, local support groups, and guidance on navigating the mental health system.

Support Groups and Peer Networks

• **MensGroup (mensgroup.com)**: An online, structured community focused on peer-led discussions, personal development, and mutual accountability for men navigating life transitions.

• **Adult Children of Alcoholics & Dysfunctional Families (ACA) (adultchildren.org)**: A peer-led twelve-step program for individuals seeking to heal from family-of-origin trauma and break chronic cycles of self-abandonment.

Immediate Crisis Support

• **The Suicide & Crisis Lifeline**: Call or text 988 (Available 24/7 in the United States and Canada). This is a free, confidential service connecting you directly to trained crisis counselors.

• **The Crisis Text Line: Text HOME to 741741** to connect with a crisis responder via text message at any hour.

Notes for Partners and Supporters

If you are reading this, you are likely a spouse, romantic partner, family member, or close friend of a man who is working his way through this 30-day action plan. You care about him, you want to see him thrive, and you have likely witnessed the toll that self-doubt, overthinking, or quiet self-abandonment has taken on his life.

Supporting a man through the process of building evidence-based self-esteem requires a delicate, high-integrity balance. It is natural to want to help, but the way you offer support can either accelerate his growth or inadvertently shut it down.

Here is a practical guide on how to walk alongside him without parenting, criticizing, or overriding his progress.

1. Shift from Parenting to Partnering

When a man is trying to rebuild his self-trust, the absolute quickest way to stall his progress is to treat him like a child who needs monitoring.

Do not police his progress: Refrain from asking, "*Did you do your five-minute practice today*?" or "*Did you keep your promise*?" Checking up on him turns his self-directed work into an obligation he owes to you, which destroys his ability to build internal accountability.

Let him hold his own baseline: If he misses a day or slips up on a promise, allow him to execute his own "clean restart." Do not step in to save him from the discomfort of a setback, and do not offer pity. Let him experience the quiet, dignified realization that he is capable of starting again on his own terms.

2. Validate the Effort, Not Just the Outcome

Because this plan is built on micro-actions, small, quiet choices rather than grand, dramatic transformations, his progress might look underwhelming from the outside.

Acknowledge the small reps: If you notice him stating a clear preference instead of going along with a plan, or if he says "no" to an extra commitment, notice it. You can say, *"I appreciate you being direct about what you need," or "I noticed you handled that situation really cleanly."*

Praise the courage, not the perfection: If he tries a new skill or joins a group and it goes awkwardly, do not try to rescue him with empty toxic positivity ("*You were the best one there*!"). Instead, validate the behavioral proof: "*You went even though you felt uncomfortable. That is what matters.*"

3. Respect His Boundaries (Even When They Challenge You)

As he moves through Chapter 6, he will begin practicing setting boundaries, stating preferences, and declining requests. This can sometimes create temporary friction in your relationship, especially if you have both grown accustomed to him passively agreeing to everything.

Allow him to say no: When he politely declines a request or states a different preference, resist the urge to negotiate, guilt-trip, or override him.

Celebrate the friction: Remind yourself that a partner who can honestly tell you "no" is a partner who can give you a trustworthy, wholehearted "yes." His boundaries are not a threat to the connection; they are the foundation of a real, unmasked relationship.

4. Step Back to Let Him Step Up

True confidence is built when a man realizes he can handle life's challenges without outsourcing his decisions.

Stop pre-emptively solving his problems: If he is venting about a work issue or a personal setback, resist the urge to jump in with advice, solutions, or a rescue plan.

Ask instead of telling: Use open-ended, respect-based questions that encourage his autonomy: "*That sounds incredibly frustrating. What do you think your next step is?*" "*How can I best support you while you figure this out?*"

By stepping back, you are sending a powerful, silent message: I believe you are capable, reliable, and strong enough to handle this. That belief is the greatest gift a supporter can offer.

References

• *Benito, K. G., & Walther, M.* (2015). Therapeutic process during exposure: Habituation model. Journal of Obsessive-Compulsive and Related Disorders, 6, 147–157. https://doi.org/10.1016/j.jocrd.2015.01.006

• *Chu, B., Marwaha, K., Sanvictores, T., Awosika, A. O., & Ayers, D.* (2024, May 7). Physiology, stress reaction. StatPearls - NCBI Bookshelf. https://www.ncbi.nlm.nih.gov/books/NBK541120/

• *Find a therapist, psychologist, counselor - Psychology today.* (n.d.). https://www.psychologytoday.com/us/therapists

• *Harvard Health.* (2024, April 3). Understanding the stress response. https://www.health.harvard.edu/staying-healthy/understanding-the-stress-response

• *Hossain, M. N., Lee, J., Choi, H., Kwak, Y., & Kim, J.* (2024). The impact of exercise on depression: how moving makes your brain and body feel better. Physical Activity and Nutrition, 28(2), 43–51. https://doi.org/10.20463/pan.2024.0015

• *Is height determined by genetics?: MedlinePlus Genetics.* (n.d.). https://medlineplus.gov/genetics/understanding/traits/height/

• *Nesh.* (2024, November 21). Stress and stress response. Strategic Psychology Canberra. https://strategicpsychology.com.au/stress-and-stress-response/

• *The steps | Adult Children of alcoholics & Dysfunctional families.* (n.d.). https://adultchildren.org/literature/steps/

• *What is ACA | Adult Children of Alcoholics & Dysfunctional Families.* (n.d.). https://adultchildren.org/newcomer/what-is-aca/

www.ingramcontent.com/pod-product-compliance
Lightning Source LLC
LaVergne TN
LVHW022219200926
848481LV00006B/2025